America Will March Forward
A primer for patriots

Other books by Arthur Milton

America Will March Forward
A primer for patriots

Arthur Milton

PATRIOT PRESS

Fort Lee, New Jersey

Published by Patriot Press
Distributed by Barricade Books Inc.
185 Bridge Plaza North
Suite 308-A
Fort Lee, NJ 07024
www.barricadebooks.com

Library of Congress Cataloging-in-Publication Data
A record of this title's Cataloging-in-Publication record can be obtained from
the Library of Congress.

ISBN 1-56980-265-3

First Printing
Manufactured in the United States of America

Dedication

This book is dedicated to the people of the United States.

All the people.

The ones in high offices. The ones who clean offices.

Those who pursue a profession at the Ivy Leagues and those who learn a skill at the vo-techs.

Small farmers, small business owners,
CEOs of large Fortune 500s.

Schoolteachers, professors, rocket scientists,
and auto mechanics.

Policemen, firemen, prison guards, and social workers.

Privates and generals. Toll takers and truckers.

Stay-at-home moms who work twenty-four-hour,
seven-day-a-week shifts.

This book is dedicated to all the good people of the United States in every highway and byway of life who toil away and give this great country its moral fiber and backbone.

It was you the Founding Fathers had in mind when they created this great and glorious nation.

Hats off to you and all the generations past and future who work to keep the United States the more perfect union it is.

CONTENTS

Prologue

Eighty years, eight decades, how much is that to the total time our great country has been in existence? I often think about that, having reached my eightieth year. Yes, the United States of America is 227 years old, July 4, the year 2003.

The events of our times concern me, as I'm sure they concern all Americans. And as I viewed my responsibilities in giving you some honest thoughts, honest in that some are most critical, I also realized that this great country became the great country that it is because down through the ages, we have had faults, and, fortunately, most of them were corrected.

So while this book is somewhat critical, it also gives a historical picture of why people came here initially, starting at Plymouth Rock, and why they still land here at all our airports from all over the world hoping that we will take them in and call them fellow citizens.

That is good because we have a lot to do in this country. First and foremost, we must continue to do what has to be done so that the very freedoms the Founding Fathers fought for will be maintained forever.

President George W. Bush has since 9/11 persevered in chasing the culprits. Notwithstanding political antagonism by some, the majority of us seem to recognize his tasks are not easy, but his accomplishments have been ever so great.

Certainly it is much too soon to judge where he and his presidency will stand in the history books. But I don't think too many will disagree that he will be placed near the top.

Part three of this book addresses the concerns I have about where the nation is today, what is wrong, and what should be done. These are issues that affect us all, the need for

- tax reform;

- better education for our children;

- eliminating bad business practices that corrupt our economy;

- a health-care system that makes us healthy;

- cleaning up our justice system to do away with the injustices that now pervade it. Our judicial system is truly costing this land of ours a fortune and is impeding progress, to which all of our citizens are entitled;

- a rebirth of civility. But that must start at home. While "road rage" has gotten many headlines, I am so concerned about the other rages, as well. There are too many that we get involved in—neighbor against neighbor, spouse against spouse, sibling against sibling. And then of course, our very democracy is inflicted with the disease of rage as some citizens rage often against others. Civility is something that we here in the United States must bring to bear not only on our 280 million fellow Americans, but throughout the world.

Making ourselves a more civil country should serve as an example to those abroad, and it is part and parcel of what we must do to fight and end terrorism at the earliest opportunity. We must remind the rest of the world that we are not their enemy, as the terrorists would have them believe. We are their beacon, the example of what can be accomplished.

Ours is a glorious history, and I emphasize glorious because students of history will tell us that no country, no world power, no one has ever had the exclusivity of a group of people that we call the Founding Fathers, the framers of our constitution, our Bill of Rights, our Declaration of Independence, and let's not forget that guy Abe who recited his Gettysburg Address. These were great men, men with a purpose, men who in the city of Philadelphia spilled out their guts day after day in the heat of the summer as they completed their work on a constitution for these United States that has lasted 227 years.

And I know when you finish reading this book, you will agree that our constitution will be there for thousands of years to come.

So read on.

PART I

From where we came

CHAPTER ONE
Colony to country

America.

It was a vast unknown, filled with dangers, disease, and hardship, "heathen and barbarous landes," as Queen Elizabeth I put it. Untamed and threatening (between 1607 and 1624, 14,000 migrated to the Virginia colony of Jamestown, only 1,132 survived), it was a land of uncertainty.

And yet they came. Some were drawn by the opportunities it was believed the New World offered. Others came to escape intolerance in the old countries. Some made the six- to twelve-week crossing, crammed into tiny ships, for sheer survival, to put food into the mouths of their family, to escape imprisonment and death.

Even back in the seventeenth century, what was to become the United States sent out a beacon of hope.

The first wave of Europeans, however, was not the settlers. They were the explorers, looking for gold and riches–which the Spanish certainly found in South and Central America–or that fabled passage to India.

Encouraged by Spain's success in the southern hemisphere, England turned its attention to North America in 1578 when the queen gave Humphrey Gilbert the nod to colonize the New World left unclaimed. Walter Raleigh took up the gauntlet and established a colony off the coast of North Carolina. That colony was a bust, as was one that came two years later. It took another twenty years before the British were ready to try again, this time in Jamestown.

It was rough going when the first group arrived in 1607. The men of the first wave were "gentlemen-adventurers" who had never done a hard day's work. They were hoping to find gold and quickly return home in glory.

Instead they were greeted by terrific heat, hostile Indians, and bugs the like of which the British Isles had never seen. When more arrived in 1609, there was no food for them.

The winter of 1609 proved disastrous. With inadequate shelter and forced to kill off the little livestock available, the settlers resorted to cannibalism. In the spring, only 60 of the 600 people had survived.

But as was to happen so many times in this country's history, out of adversity came enterprise. A new arrival, John Rolfe, did some experimenting in agriculture and developed a tobacco strain palatable to European tastes. In 1614, the first shipload of Virginia tobacco reached London, bringing prosperity to another corner of the New World.

The Virginia settlers were, as it turned out, the first trickle of immigrants that eventually turned into a tidal wave lasting four centuries right up until today.

* * *

In the north, it was not the siren call of gold that lured the early arrivals. For the Pilgrims, it was the possibility of being left alone.

The 1500s and early 1600s was a time of religious displacement and upheaval in Europe as Protestants struggled with the ramifications of Martin Luther nailing his grievances against the Catholic Church on a church door in Wittenberg, Germany.

Not surprisingly, Protestantism lacked the unity of Rome, and it took little time before movements sprung up with divergent theologies. As is often the case, the majority sector did not allow dissent. The Church of England, for one, refused to recognize–as some very wise fellows did following the American Revolution–that strength lies in allowing opposing ideas, not in attempting to quash them.

The Puritans were a group that broke ranks with the Church of England. While their views were religious, they also had political ramifications. Was the monarchy a waystop on the road to God? Should the king or queen have divine rights? Or was it a straight shot from the individual to God?

The Puritans believed the latter, and that didn't sit well with the throne. In 1608 one group of Separatists, as they were called, left the unfriendly climes of England for the more-tolerant Holland. There they were granted full religious freedom, but interestingly, after twelve years, the Puritans feared their children were being corrupted by Dutch society. A group, dubbed Pilgrims, decided to make a go of it in the New World. They were granted territory in Virginia by the London Company.

The sixty-five-day voyage of the *Mayflower* began September 16, 1602. Off course, either by fate or design, the Pilgrims came within sight of Cape Cod, eventually landing in Plymouth December 21.

That change of course had a significant consequence. Since the settlers were not under the province of the London Company, with its laws and strictures, that left the necessity of forming a government of their own. And so it was that the Mayflower Compact was drawn, promising "just and equal laws."

Even though "just and equal" would pertain only to other Puritans, it was the first baby step towards our more perfect union. It would lead to Roger Williams throwing up his hands at the rigid Puritan orthodoxy and the seizure of Indian lands. Banished, he bought some land from natives in what is now Rhode Island and set up the first colony with complete separation of church and state and the freedom to worship as one pleased.

The rest of the century saw a jockeying to set up more colonies–the Dutch in New York with its patroon system, the Swedes along the Delaware River, the Quakers and other religious dissenters under the auspices of William Penn in Pennsylvania–that stretched down to South Carolina.

Each outburst in Europe and England of religious persecution, economic hardship and civil unrest brought another wave of immigrants to the Promised Land.

* * *

While those early colonists were a mixed bag, they had some things in common. Among them were a spirit of independence and a propensity to challenge the status quo if it wasn't to their liking.

Furthermore, the great distance from London meant local control, and the colonists took a liking to being in charge of their destinies. You're talking about a bunch of tough individualists.

It was to be these qualities that proved the undoing of the Crown.

With the ouster of the Dutch from New York and the defeat of the French, England had cemented its rule over the colonies. The colonists who fought in support of England in the French and Indian War of 1763 figured the grateful motherland would start cutting them some economic slack. But the king felt he had the right, the divine right, to call the shots and so dispatched an army to "protect" the colonists.

The colonists, however, viewed this as a preemptive move to put down any possible rebellion. To exacerbate the ill feelings, King George III decreed that the colonies would pay for the army.

Then there was the question of those vexing acts emanating from London. Like the one that said all foreign goods on their way to the colonies had to go through British ports. Or that infuriating high tariff on sugar grown in the French West Indies, forcing colonists to purchase the more-expensive British West Indies sugar. Yes, let us not forget the ever-so-popular Stamp Act, the first direct tax on colonists, which went into effect November 1, 1765. All printed material, from newspapers to playing cards, had to bear an official stamp, which ranged in price from a halfpenny to ten pounds.

There were those in the colonies that took exception to "taxation without representation."

Virginian Patrick Henry, for one. He suggested in no uncertain terms that only that colony's House of Burgesses had the right to impose taxes there. And just to be sure he had the attention of King George, he added, "If this be treason, make the most of it."

Fighting words, to be sure. And to drive them home, an underground group called the Sons of Liberty was formed. Its members burned stamps, harassed agents, and did what they could to prevent the collection of the taxes. Sam Adams, leader of the Boston branch of the Sons of Liberty, railed against the act and even hung a "stamp agent" puppet to a tree, which became known as the Liberty Tree. Colonists across the board refused to pay the tax.

King George didn't take the hint. If the Stamp Act was a bust in collecting revenue, the thinking in Parliament was try, try again. And so it was that the Townshend Acts were passed in June 1767. All goods shipped to the colonies from England–paper, tea, paint, you name it–would be taxed. Furthermore, a board of custom collectors was established, further diminishing local control.

What the powers-that-were in London hadn't counted on was a boycott. To raise revenue from an import tax, the colonists had to buy the imports. Instead, they respectfully and sometimes not so respectfully, declined to do so.

Parliament finally threw in the towel in March 1770. But instead of admitting complete defeat, it repealed everything but the tax on tea. Not the best decision that august body ever made.

Tensions escalated, incidents occurred, such as the "Boston Massacre" of March 5, 1770, where British soldiers fired on a crowd, killing three and wounding eight. This was followed by the Boston Tea Party in 1773, after a new tax on tea was imposed.

The latter incident infuriated King George and Parliament, leading to the "Intolerance Acts," meant to teach the colonist hooligans a lesson. No town meetings. More troops. Closing the port of Boston.

But rather than douse the flames of resistance, these punitive measures united the other colonies in support of Massachusetts.

No matter what is taught in American elementary schools, the first true shot of the Revolutionary War was not fired on Breed or Bunker Hill. It came at the sounding of the gavel that opened the first Continental Congress in Philadelphia in 1774. It would bring together George Washington, John and Samuel Adams, Patrick Henry and John Jay, and other great men in the upcoming fight for independence.

Not that the fifty-six delegates intended this meeting to be the beginning of such a battle. Rather they wished to lay out their grievances, proclaim that Parliament had trampled the rights of the colonists, and ask that those rights be restored. To put some weight behind their words, the delegates voted to boycott British goods.

Britain's response? Punish the upstarts by keeping them from the

North Atlantic fishing grounds. Force them to trade only with the mother country and the British West Indies. After all, might makes right. Britain had three times the population of the colonies, one of the, if not the, strongest navies in the world, and a well-trained professional army. The thirteen colonies were disorganized and distrustful of each other with no army to speak of.

But what Britain didn't count on was the mettle of the people of the colonies, like firebrand Patrick Henry who proclaimed, "Give me liberty or give me death." His words became a rallying cry.

Given the colonists' passion and the Crown's intractability, it was inevitable that war would follow.

And so it did with the "shot heard round the world" at the battle of Concord in April 1775. The convening of the Second Continental Congress in May 1775 was to mark a pivotal point in the upcoming war of independence. George Washington, a hero of the French and Indian War, was named commander of a to-be-formed Continental army. The die had been cast.

Thomas Paine sounded the call in his "Common Sense" pamphlet that America was obliged morally to be independent and democratic, a concept so alien in world history and yet to be the cornerstone of our union.

It became clear that the destiny of the colonies did not lie with kings and queens. There could be no compromise. It was to be liberty or death.

And so it was, under the leadership of Thomas Jefferson, that a declaration of independence was composed with words that still ring across the decades with power and wisdom.

"When in the course of human events, it becomes necessary for one people to dissolve the political bands which have connected them with another....

"... We hold these truths to be self-evident, that all men are created equal."

* * *

Thrust and parry finally led to outright combat.

It would be easy to view the Revolutionary War as a scoreboard, a body and battle count.

English: New York, Georgia, South Carolina.

Patriots: Trenton, Princeton, Saratoga.

Of course, it's always the final score that counts. In that war, our war, it was the last battle. The brilliant strategy to force General Cornwallis into a classic pincer on the Virginia peninsula of Yorktown. Trapped by land, no navy to rescue his army with its mercenary German Hessians by sea marked the end of the military struggle.

However, the true victory of the Revolutionary War was not won in battle. Rather it was won in the minds of the disparate personalities of Washington, Adams, Jefferson, Hamilton, and all the others who fought each other and in the end compromised to forge the alliance creating the nation we now know as the United States of America. And the most important word in that new name was one Thomas Paine introduced— "united."

The Declaration of Independence of the Thirteen Colonies
In CONGRESS, July 4, 1776

The unanimous Declaration of the thirteen united States of America,

When in the Course of human events, it becomes necessary for one people to dissolve the political bands which have connected them with another, and to assume among the powers of the earth, the separate and equal station to which the Laws of Nature and of Nature's God entitle them, a decent respect to the opinions of mankind requires that they should declare the causes which impel them to the separation.

We hold these truths to be self-evident, that all men are created equal, that they are endowed by their Creator with certain unalienable Rights, that among these are Life, Liberty and the pursuit of Happiness. —That to secure these rights, Governments are instituted among Men, deriving their just powers from the consent of the gov-

erned, – That whenever any Form of Government becomes destructive of these ends, it is the Right of the People to alter or to abolish it, and to institute new Government, laying its foundation on such principles and organizing its powers in such form, as to them shall seem most likely to effect their Safety and Happiness. Prudence, indeed, will dictate that Governments long established should not be changed for light and transient causes; and accordingly all experience hath shewn, that mankind are more disposed to suffer, while evils are sufferable, than to right themselves by abolishing the forms to which they are accustomed. But when a long train of abuses and usurpations, pursuing invariably the same Object evinces a design to reduce them under absolute Despotism, it is their right, it is their duty, to throw off such Government, and to provide new Guards for their future security. – Such has been the patient sufferance of these Colonies; and such is now the necessity which constrains them to alter their former Systems of Government. The history of the present King of Great Britain [George III] is a history of repeated injuries and usurpations, all having in direct object the establishment of an absolute Tyranny over these States. To prove this, let Facts be submitted to a candid world.

He has refused his Assent to Laws, the most wholesome and necessary for the public good.

He has forbidden his Governors to pass Laws of immediate and pressing importance, unless suspended in their operation till his Assent should be obtained; and when so suspended, he has utterly neglected to attend to them.

He has refused to pass other Laws for the accommodation of large districts of people, unless those people would relinquish the right of Representation in the Legislature, a right inestimable to them and formidable to tyrants only.

He has called together legislative bodies at places unusual, uncomfortable, and distant from the depository of their public Records, for the sole purpose of fatiguing them into compliance with his measures.

He has dissolved Representative Houses repeatedly, for opposing with manly firmness his invasions on the rights of the people.

He has refused for a long time, after such dissolutions, to cause others to be elected; whereby the Legislative powers, incapable of Annihilation, have returned to the People at large for their exercise; the State remaining in the mean time exposed to all the dangers of invasion from without, and convulsions within.

He has endeavoured to prevent the population of these States; for that purpose obstructing the Laws for Naturalization of Foreigners; refusing to pass others to encourage their migrations hither, and raising the conditions of new Appropriations of Lands.

He has obstructed the Administration of Justice, by refusing his Assent to Laws for establishing Judiciary powers.

He has made Judges dependent on his Will alone, for the tenure of their offices, and the amount and payment of their salaries.

He has erected a multitude of New Offices, and sent hither swarms of Officers to harass our people, and eat out their substance.

He has kept among us, in times of peace, Standing Armies without the consent of our legislatures.

He has affected to render the Military independent of and superior to the Civil power.

He has combined with others to subject us to a jurisdiction foreign to our constitution and unacknowledged by our laws; giving his Assent to their Acts of pretended Legislation:

For Quartering large bodies of armed troops among us:

For protecting them, by a mock Trial, from punishment for any Murders which they should commit on the Inhabitants of these States:

For cutting off our Trade with all parts of the world:

For imposing Taxes on us without our Consent:

For depriving us, in many cases, of the benefits of Trial by Jury:

For transporting us beyond Seas to be tried for pretended offences:

For abolishing the free System of English Laws in a neighbouring Province, establishing therein an Arbitrary government, and enlarging its Boundaries so as to render it at once an example and fit instrument for introducing the same absolute rule into these Colonies:

For taking away our Charters, abolishing our most valuable Laws, and altering fundamentally the Forms of our Governments:

For suspending our own Legislatures, and declaring themselves invested with power to legislate for us in all cases whatsoever.

He has abdicated Government here, by declaring us out of his Protection and waging War against us.

He has plundered our seas, ravaged our Coasts, burnt our towns, and destroyed the lives of our people.

He is at this time transporting large Armies of foreign Mercenaries to compleat the works of death, desolation and tyranny, already begun with circumstances of Cruelty and perfidy scarcely paralleled in the most barbarous ages, and totally unworthy the Head of a civilized nation.

He has constrained our fellow Citizens taken Captive on the high Seas to bear Arms against their Country, to become the executioners of their friends and Brethren, or to fall themselves by their Hands.

He has excited domestic insurrections amongst us, and has endeavoured to bring on the inhabitants of our frontiers, the merciless Indian Savages, whose known rule of warfare, is an undistinguished destruction of all ages, sexes and conditions.

In every stage of these Oppressions We have Petitioned for Redress in the most humble terms: Our repeated Petitions have been answered only by repeated injury. A Prince whose character is thus marked by every act which may define a Tyrant, is unfit to be the ruler of a free people.

Nor have We been wanting in attentions to our British brethren. We have warned them from time to time of attempts by their legislature to extend an unwarrantable jurisdiction over us. We have reminded them of the circumstances of our emigration and settlement here. We have appealed to their native justice and magnanimity, and we have conjured them by the ties of our common kindred to disavow these usurpations, which, would inevitably interrupt our connections and correspondence. They too have been deaf to the voice of justice and of consanguinity. We must, therefore, acquiesce in the necessity, which denounces our Separation, and hold them, as we hold the rest of mankind, Enemies in War, in Peace Friends.

We, therefore, the Representatives of the united States of America, in General Congress, Assembled, appealing to the Supreme Judge of the world for the rectitude of our intentions, do, in the Name, and by the Authority of the good People of these Colonies, solemnly publish and declare, That these United Colonies are, and of Right ought to be Free and Independent States; that they are Absolved from all Allegiance to the British Crown, and that all political connection between them and the State of Great Britain, is and ought to be totally dissolved; and that as Free and Independent States, they have full Power to levy War, conclude Peace, contract Alliances, establish Commerce, and to do all other Acts and Things which Independent States may of right do. And for the support of this Declaration, with a firm reliance on the protection of divine Providence, we mutually pledge to each other our Lives, our Fortunes and our sacred Honor.

CHAPTER TWO
Creating a more perfect union

So what did these guys, the men we call the Founding Fathers, actually wrought? What was it they had in mind that created this flawed, but closer to perfect system of government–transformed into a system of society–than has ever existed in the history of mankind?

To understand their mind-set, first off you have to understand their time as opposed to ours. The Dow Jones and MTV were not on their radarscope–radar wasn't on their radarscope, for that matter. These were men who read and thought and were full of ideas.

Then you have to realize they were the children of an era of extreme intellectual excitement–the Enlightenment. The crew of the starship Enterprise might be going "where no man has gone before" in its fictional exploration of outer space, but the great philosophers of the Enlightenment were on an even-more perilous adventure. They were pushing the boundaries of thoughts, ideas, and concepts.

Out of the Enlightenment came the notion that, hey, just because someone was born a Stewart or a Tudor that didn't give King George III the divine right to tell the colonists what to do. Jefferson, Madison, Adams, Franklin read and studied the great thinkers of the Enlightenment–John Locke, the baron de Montesquieu, David Hume–and concluded they put forward great principles on which to build a country.

Take Locke, whom Thomas Jefferson deemed one of the three "greatest men that have ever lived, without exception." Locke said phooey to the notion of divine right of kings, arguing it wasn't natural. Men were born free and equal. Government, which is nothing more than a social contract with its citizens, should protect life, liberty, and property. Just as revolutionary, Locke maintained that in most things, majority opinion should carry the day.

15

All fine words and concepts, but Locke went further. He proposed a system of government, one that inspired the Founding Fathers. Separate powers between three branches—executive, legislative, and federative—and build into the system checks and balances so that one branch would not dominate the others, leading to tyranny and suppression.

Montesquieu expanded on the concept of balance of power and changed the third branch to the judiciary. He wrote, "When the [law-making] and [law-enforcement] powers are united in the same person—there can be no liberty."

Hume, who believed that politics could be studied as a science, and Locke were inspired by the New World. They saw it expanding wealth and opportunity. Their theories of government, which so profoundly influenced the framing of the American constitution, were tremendously optimistic because of the New World.

Both were strong proponents of the right to private property. Hume went so far as to say that without private property there could be no justice. In a famous analysis, Locke asked who owned the nuts in a great forest? Well, he reasoned, they don't belong to anyone. (This was in the days when there was still untitled land.) However, he continued, when someone used effort to gather the nuts, they belonged to that person because work has value.

Hume's argument that private property is necessary for justice is laced throughout the U.S. constitution. If you work hard, gather enough nuts, you deserve to become the Nut King. Government and kings should not have the right to capriciously levy taxes or claim ownership of land and output.

None of this is to say that the Founding Fathers were guilty of gross plagiarism. Their greatness lies in recognizing that the Enlightenment thinkers had hit on principles on which to build a country. They used Enlightenment philosophies for constructing institutions of government.

It is extraordinary that the Founding Fathers did such a good job that the system still works as they conceived it. Consider the fact that during the same time we have had one constitution, France—today in its fifth republic—has had twenty-three! It's quite amazing to think that these men

16

of the American constitutional convention were able to create a government based on seventeenth- and eighteenth-century philosophy that still works in the twenty-first.

The constitution is an exceptional document, especially considering these fellows were flying by the seat of their pants. This was the first reasoned, written plan for government. It did not evolve over centuries, as did the British parliamentary system. This was a bunch of guys, rolling up their sleeves in the smothering heat of a Philadelphia summer, and saying, "Let's do it. Let's figure out something that's going to work."

A reading of the constitution is evidence of the fine level of detail and thought that went into its construction. The framers attempted–and did a damned good job–to cover all the bases.

How old should a presidential candidate be? Who gets to pass taxes? Make treaties? What constitutes treason? Who passes laws? Interprets them. And when enough is enough, how do you get the rascals out of office?

Article after article, section after section, clause after clause, a new form of government was constructed through argument and compromise. The Electoral College was thrown in so that the bigger states would not always hold sway over the smaller, a way to level the voting field.

The concept of amendments was included so that the constitution could change with changing times, adapt to necessity, and keep it flexible.

Still there were those who adamantly opposed the constitution. To them, a strong central government was the path to tyranny. The opponents attacked the document as vague, lacking specific delineation of "those essential rights of mankind without which liberty cannot exist."

On the other side of the argument, proponents said state constitutions already guaranteed individual rights. But in the end, bill of rights advocates prevailed. And so, almost immediately, the wisdom of including a way to change the constitution was proven correct. The first ten amendments, known as the Bill of Rights, came into being.

We the people of the United States, in order to form a more perfect union, establish justice, insure domestic tranquility, provide for the

17

common defense, promote the general welfare, and secure the blessings of liberty to ourselves and our posterity, do ordain and establish this Constitution for the United States of America.

Article I

Section 1. All legislative powers herein granted shall be vested in a Congress of the United States, which shall consist of a Senate and House of Representatives.

Section 2. The House of Representatives shall be composed of members chosen every second year by the people of the several states, and the electors in each state shall have the qualifications requisite for electors of the most numerous branch of the state legislature.

No person shall be a Representative who shall not have attained to the age of twenty five years, and been seven years a citizen of the United States, and who shall not, when elected, be an inhabitant of that state in which he shall be chosen.

Representatives and direct taxes shall be apportioned among the several states which may be included within this union, according to their respective numbers, which shall be determined by adding to the whole number of free persons, including those bound to service for a term of years, and excluding Indians not taxed, three fifths of all other Persons. The actual Enumeration shall be made within three years after the first meeting of the Congress of the United States, and within every subsequent term of ten years, in such manner as they shall by law direct. The number of Representatives shall not exceed one for every thirty thousand, but each state shall have at least one Representative; and until such enumeration shall be made, the state of New Hampshire shall be entitled to chuse three, Massachusetts eight, Rhode Island and Providence Plantations one, Connecticut five, New York six, New Jersey four, Pennsylvania eight, Delaware one, Maryland six, Virginia ten, North Carolina five, South Carolina five, and Georgia three.

When vacancies happen in the Representation from any state, the executive authority thereof shall issue writs of election to fill such vacancies.

The House of Representatives shall choose their speaker and other officers; and shall have the sole power of impeachment.

Section 3. The Senate of the United States shall be composed of two Senators from each state, chosen by the legislature thereof, for six years; and each Senator shall have one vote.

Immediately after they shall be assembled in consequence of the first election, they shall be divided as equally as may be into three classes. The seats of the Senators of the first class shall be vacated at the expiration of the second year, of the second class at the expiration of the fourth year, and the third class at the expiration of the sixth year, so that one third may be chosen every second year; and if vacancies happen by resignation, or otherwise, during the recess of the legislature of any state, the executive thereof may make temporary appointments until the next meeting of the legislature, which shall then fill such vacancies.

No person shall be a Senator who shall not have attained to the age of thirty years, and been nine years a citizen of the United States and who shall not, when elected, be an inhabitant of that state for which he shall be chosen.

The Vice President of the United States shall be President of the Senate, but shall have no vote, unless they be equally divided.

The Senate shall choose their other officers, and also a President pro tempore, in the absence of the Vice President, or when he shall exercise the office of President of the United States.

The Senate shall have the sole power to try all impeachments. When sitting for that purpose, they shall be on oath or affirmation. When the President of the United States is tried, the Chief Justice shall preside: And no person shall be convicted without the concurrence of two thirds of the members present.

Judgment in cases of impeachment shall not extend further than to removal from office, and disqualification to hold and enjoy any office of honor, trust or profit under the United States: but the party convicted shall nevertheless be liable and subject to indictment, trial, judgment and punishment, according to law.

Section 4. The times, places and manner of holding elections for Senators and Representatives, shall be prescribed in each state by the legislature thereof; but the Congress may at any time by law make or alter such regulations, except as to the places of choosing Senators.

The Congress shall assemble at least once in every year, and such meeting shall be on the first Monday in December, unless they shall by law appoint a different day.

Section 5. Each House shall be the judge of the elections, returns and qualifications of its own members, and a majority of each shall constitute a quorum to do business; but a smaller number may adjourn from day to day, and may be authorized to compel the attendance of absent members, in such manner, and under such penalties as each House may provide.

Each House may determine the rules of its proceedings, punish its members for disorderly behavior, and, with the concurrence of two thirds, expel a member.

Each House shall keep a journal of its proceedings, and from time to time publish the same, excepting such parts as may in their judgment require secrecy; and the yeas and nays of the members of either House on any question shall, at the desire of one fifth of those present, be entered on the journal.

Neither House, during the session of Congress, shall, without the consent of the other, adjourn for more than three days, nor to any other place than that in which the two Houses shall be sitting.

Section 6. The Senators and Representatives shall receive a compensation for their services, to be ascertained by law, and paid out of the treasury of the United States. They shall in all cases, except treason, felony and breach of the peace, be privileged from arrest during their attendance at the session of their respective Houses, and in going to and returning from the same; and for any speech or debate in either House, they shall not be questioned in any other place.

No Senator or Representative shall, during the time for which he was elected, be appointed to any civil office under the authority of the United States, which shall have been created, or the emoluments whereof shall have been increased during such time: and no person holding any office under the United States, shall be a member of either House during his continuance in office.

Section 7. All bills for raising revenue shall originate in the House of Representatives; but the Senate may propose or concur with amendments as on other Bills.

Every bill which shall have passed the House of Representatives and the Senate, shall, before it become a law, be presented to the President of the United States; if he approve he shall sign it, but if not he shall return it, with his objections to that House in which it shall have originated, who shall enter the objections at large on their journal, and proceed to reconsider it. If after such reconsideration two thirds of that House shall agree to pass the bill, it shall be sent, together with the objections, to the other House, by which it shall likewise be reconsidered, and if approved by two thirds of that House, it shall become a law. But in all such cases the votes of both Houses shall be determined by yeas and nays, and the names of the persons voting for and against the bill shall be entered on the journal of each House respectively. If any bill shall not be returned by the President within ten days (Sundays excepted) after it shall have been presented to him, the same shall be a law, in like manner as if he had signed it, unless the Congress by their adjournment prevent its return, in which case it shall not be a law.

Every order, resolution, or vote to which the concurrence of the Senate and House of Representatives may be necessary (except on a question of adjournment) shall be presented to the President of the United States; and before the same shall take effect, shall be approved by him, or being disapproved by him, shall be repassed by two thirds of the Senate and House of Representatives, according to the rules and limitations prescribed in the case of a bill.

Section 8. The Congress shall have power to lay and collect taxes, duties, imposts and excises, to pay the debts and provide for the common defense and general welfare of the United States; but all duties, imposts and excises shall be uniform throughout the United States;

To borrow money on the credit of the United States;

To regulate commerce with foreign nations, and among the several states, and with the Indian tribes;

To establish a uniform rule of naturalization, and uniform laws on the subject of bankruptcies throughout the United States;

To coin money, regulate the value thereof, and of foreign coin, and fix the standard of weights and measures;

To provide for the punishment of counterfeiting the securities and current coin of the United States;

To establish post offices and post roads;

To promote the progress of science and useful arts, by securing for limited times to authors and inventors the exclusive right to their respective writings and discoveries;

To constitute tribunals inferior to the Supreme Court;

To define and punish piracies and felonies committed on the high seas, and offenses against the law of nations;

To declare war, grant letters of marque and reprisal, and make rules concerning captures on land and water;

To raise and support armies, but no appropriation of money to that use shall be for a longer term than two years;

To provide and maintain a navy;

To make rules for the government and regulation of the land and naval forces;

To provide for calling forth the militia to execute the laws of the union, suppress insurrections and repel invasions;

To provide for organizing, arming, and disciplining, the militia, and for governing such part of them as may be employed in the service of the United States, reserving to the states respectively, the appointment of the officers, and the authority of training the militia according to the discipline prescribed by Congress;

To exercise exclusive legislation in all cases whatsoever, over such District (not exceeding ten miles square) as may, by cession of particular states, and the acceptance of Congress, become the seat of the government of the United States, and to exercise like authority over all places purchased by the consent of the legislature of the state in which the same shall be, for the erection of forts, magazines, arsenals, dockyards, and other needful buildings;–And

To make all laws which shall be necessary and proper for carrying into execution the foregoing powers, and all other powers vested by this Constitution in the government of the United States, or in any department or officer thereof.

Section 9. The migration or importation of such persons as any of the states now existing shall think proper to admit, shall not be pro-

hibited by the Congress prior to the year one thousand eight hundred and eight, but a tax or duty may be imposed on such importation, not exceeding ten dollars for each person.

The privilege of the writ of habeas corpus shall not be suspended, unless when in cases of rebellion or invasion the public safety may require it.

No bill of attainder or ex post facto Law shall be passed.

No capitation, or other direct, tax shall be laid, unless in proportion to the census or enumeration herein before directed to be taken.

No tax or duty shall be laid on articles exported from any state.

No preference shall be given by any regulation of commerce or revenue to the ports of one state over those of another: nor shall vessels bound to, or from, one state, be obliged to enter, clear or pay duties in another.

No money shall be drawn from the treasury, but in consequence of appropriations made by law; and a regular statement and account of receipts and expenditures of all public money shall be published from time to time.

No title of nobility shall be granted by the United States: and no person holding any office of profit or trust under them, shall, without the consent of the Congress, accept of any present, emolument, office, or title, of any kind whatever, from any king, prince, or foreign state.

Section 10. No state shall enter into any treaty, alliance, or confederation; grant letters of marque and reprisal; coin money; emit bills of credit; make anything but gold and silver coin a tender in payment of debts; pass any bill of attainder, ex post facto law, or law impairing the obligation of contracts, or grant any title of nobility.

No state shall, without the consent of the Congress, lay any imposts or duties on imports or exports, except what may be absolutely necessary for executing its inspection laws: and the net produce of all duties and imposts, laid by any state on imports or exports, shall be for the use of the treasury of the United States; and all such laws shall be subject to the revision and control of the Congress.

No state shall, without the consent of Congress, lay any duty of tonnage, keep troops, or ships of war in time of peace, enter into any agreement or compact with another state, or with a foreign power, or *engage in war, unless actually invaded, or in such imminent danger as will not admit of delay.*

Article II

Section 1. The executive power shall be vested in a President of the United States of America. He shall hold his office during the term of four years, and, together with the Vice President, chosen for the same term, be elected, as follows:

Each state shall appoint, in such manner as the Legislature thereof may direct, a number of electors, equal to the whole number of Senators and Representatives to which the State may be entitled in the Congress: but no Senator or Representative, or person holding an office of trust or profit under the United States, shall be appointed an elector.

The electors shall meet in their respective states, and vote by ballot for two persons, of whom one at least shall not be an inhabitant of the same state with themselves. And they shall make a list of all the persons voted for, and of the number of votes for each; which list they shall sign and certify, and transmit sealed to the seat of the government of the United States, directed to the President of the Senate. The President of the Senate shall, in the presence of the Senate and House of Representatives, open all the certificates, and the votes shall then be counted. The person having the greatest number of votes shall be the President, if such number be a majority of the whole number of electors appointed; and if there be more than one who have such majority, and have an equal number of votes, then the House of Representatives shall immediately choose by ballot one of them for President; and if no person have a majority, then from the five highest on the list the said House shall in like manner choose the President. But in choosing the President, the votes shall be taken by States, the representation from each state having one vote; A quorum for this purpose shall consist of a member or members from two thirds of the states, and a majority of all the states shall be necessary to a choice. In every case, after the choice of the President, the person having the greatest number of votes of the electors shall be the Vice President. But if there should remain two or more who have equal votes, the Senate shall choose from them by ballot the Vice President.

The Congress may determine the time of choosing the electors, and the day on which they shall give their votes; which day shall be the same throughout the United States.

No person except a natural born citizen, or a citizen of the United States, at the time of the adoption of this Constitution, shall be eligible to the office of President; neither shall any person be eligible to that office who shall not have attained to the age of thirty five years, and been fourteen Years a resident within the United States.

In case of the removal of the President from office, or of his death, resignation, or inability to discharge the powers and duties of the said office, the same shall devolve on the Vice President, and the Congress may by law provide for the case of removal, death, resignation or inability, both of the President and Vice President, declaring what officer shall then act as President, and such officer shall act accordingly, until the disability be removed, or a President shall be elected.

The President shall, at stated times, receive for his services, a compensation, which shall neither be increased nor diminished during the period for which he shall have been elected, and he shall not receive within that period any other emolument from the United States, or any of them.

Before he enter on the execution of his office, he shall take the following oath or affirmation:—"I do solemnly swear (or affirm) that I will faithfully execute the office of President of the United States, and will to the best of my ability, preserve, protect and defend the Constitution of the United States."

Section 2. The President shall be commander in chief of the Army and Navy of the United States, and of the militia of the several states, when called into the actual service of the United States; he may require the opinion, in writing, of the principal officer in each of the executive departments, upon any subject relating to the duties of their respective offices, and he shall have power to grant reprieves and pardons for offenses against the United States, except in cases of impeachment.

He shall have power, by and with the advice and consent of the Senate, to make treaties, provided two thirds of the Senators present concur; and he shall nominate, and by and with the advice and consent of the Senate, shall appoint ambassadors, other public ministers and consuls, judges of the Supreme Court, and all other officers of the United States, whose appointments are not herein otherwise provided *for, and which shall be established by law: but the Congress may by law vest the appointment of such inferior officers, as they think proper, in the President alone, in the courts of law, or in the heads of departments.*

The President shall have power to fill up all vacancies that may happen during the recess of the Senate, by granting commissions which shall expire at the end of their next session.

Section 3. He shall from time to time give to the Congress information of the state of the union, and recommend to their consideration such measures as he shall judge necessary and expedient; he may, on extraordinary occasions, convene both Houses, or either of them, and in case of disagreement between them, with respect to the time of adjournment, he may adjourn them to such time as he shall think proper; he shall receive ambassadors and other public ministers; he shall take care that the laws be faithfully executed, and shall commission all the officers of the United States.

Section 4. The President, Vice President and all civil officers of the United States, shall be removed from office on impeachment for, and conviction of, treason, bribery, or other high crimes and misdemeanors.

Article III

Section 1. The judicial power of the United States, shall be vested in one Supreme Court, and in such inferior courts as the Congress may from time to time ordain and establish. The judges, both of the supreme and inferior courts, shall hold their offices during good behaviour, and shall, at stated times, receive for their services, a compensation, which shall not be diminished during their continuance in office.

Section 2. The judicial power shall extend to all cases, in law and equity, arising under this Constitution, the laws of the United States, and treaties made, or which shall be made, under their authority;—to all cases affecting ambassadors, other public ministers and consuls;—to all cases of admiralty and maritime jurisdiction;—to controversies to which the United States shall be a party;—to controversies between two or more states;—between a state and citizens of another state;—between citizens of different states;—between citizens of the same state claiming lands under grants of different states, and between a state, or the citizens thereof, and foreign states, citizens or subjects.

In all cases affecting ambassadors, other public ministers and consuls, and those in which a state shall be party, the Supreme Court shall have original jurisdiction. In all the other cases before mentioned, the Supreme Court shall have appellate jurisdiction, both as to law and fact, with such exceptions, and under such regulations as the Congress shall make.

The trial of all crimes, except in cases of impeachment, shall be by jury; and such trial shall be held in the state where the said crimes shall have been committed; but when not committed within any state, the trial shall be at such place or places as the Congress may by law have directed.

Section 3. Treason against the United States, shall consist only in levying war against them, or in adhering to their enemies, giving them aid and comfort. No person shall be convicted of treason unless on the testimony of two witnesses to the same overt act, or on confession in open court.

The Congress shall have power to declare the punishment of treason, but no attainder of treason shall work corruption of blood, or forfeiture except during the life of the person attainted.

Article IV

Section 1. Full faith and credit shall be given in each state to the public acts, records, and judicial proceedings of every other state. And the Congress may by general laws prescribe the manner in which such acts, records, and proceedings shall be proved, and the effect thereof.

Section 2. The citizens of each state shall be entitled to all privileges and immunities of citizens in the several states.

A person charged in any state with treason, felony, or other crime, who shall flee from justice, and be found in another state, shall on demand of the executive authority of the state from which he fled, be delivered up, to be removed to the state having jurisdiction of the crime.

No person held to service or labor in one state, under the laws thereof, escaping into another, shall, in consequence of any law or regulation therein, be discharged from such service or labor, but shall be delivered up on claim of the party to whom such service or labor may be due.

Section 3. New states may be admitted by the Congress into this union; but no new states shall be formed or erected within the jurisdiction of any other state; nor any state be formed by the junction of two or more states, or parts of states, without the consent of the legislatures of the states concerned as well as of the Congress.

The Congress shall have power to dispose of and make all needful rules and regulations respecting the territory or other property belonging to the United States; and nothing in this Constitution shall be so construed as to prejudice any claims of the United States, or of any particular state.

Section 4. The United States shall guarantee to every state in this union a republican form of government, and shall protect each of them against invasion; and on application of the legislature, or of the executive (when the legislature cannot be convened) against domestic violence.

Article V

The Congress, whenever two thirds of both houses shall deem it necessary, shall propose amendments to this Constitution, or, on the application of the legislatures of two thirds of the several states, shall call a convention for proposing amendments, which, in either case, shall be valid to all intents and purposes, as part of this Constitution, when ratified by the legislatures of three fourths of the several states, or by conventions in three fourths thereof, as the one or the other mode of ratification may be proposed by the Congress; provided that no amendment which may be made prior to the year one thousand eight hundred and eight shall in any manner affect the first and fourth clauses in the ninth section of the first article; and that no state, without its consent, shall be deprived of its equal suffrage in the Senate.

Article VI

All debts contracted and engagements entered into, before the adoption of this Constitution, shall be as valid against the United States under this Constitution, as under the Confederation.

This Constitution, and the laws of the United States which shall be made in pursuance thereof; and all treaties made, or which shall be made, under the authority of the United States, shall be the supreme law of the land; and the judges in every state shall be bound thereby, anything in the Constitution or laws of any State to the contrary notwithstanding.

The Senators and Representatives before mentioned, and the members of the several state legislatures, and all executive and judicial officers, both of the United States and of the several states, shall be bound by oath or affirmation, to support this Constitution; but no religious test shall ever be required as a qualification to any office or public trust under the United States.

Article VII

The ratification of the conventions of nine states, shall be sufficient for the establishment of this Constitution between the states so ratifying the same.

Done in convention by the unanimous consent of the states present the seventeenth day of September in the year of our Lord one thousand seven hundred and eighty seven and of the independence of the United States of America the twelfth.

Bill of Rights

Amendment I

Congress shall make no law respecting an establishment of religion, or prohibiting the free exercise thereof; or abridging the freedom of speech, or of the press; or the right of the people peaceably to assemble, and to petition the government for a redress of grievances.

Amendment II

A well regulated militia, being necessary to the security of a free state, the right of the people to keep and bear arms, shall not be infringed.

Amendment III

No soldier shall, in time of peace be quartered in any house, without the consent of the owner, nor in time of war, but in a manner to be prescribed by law.

Amendment IV

The right of the people to be secure in their persons, houses, papers, and effects, against unreasonable searches and seizures, shall not be violated, and no warrants shall issue, but upon probable cause, supported by oath or affirmation, and particularly describing the place to be searched, and the persons or things to be seized.

Amendment V

No person shall be held to answer for a capital, or otherwise infamous crime, unless on a presentment or indictment of a grand jury, except in cases arising in the land or naval forces, or in the militia, when in actual service in time of war or public danger; nor shall any person be subject for the same offense to be twice put in jeopardy of life or limb; nor shall be compelled in any criminal case to be a witness against himself, nor be deprived of life, liberty, or property, without due process of law; nor shall private property be taken for public use, without just compensation.

Amendment VI

In all criminal prosecutions, the accused shall enjoy the right to a speedy and public trial, by an impartial jury of the state and district wherein the crime shall have been committed, which district shall have been previously ascertained by law, and to be informed of the nature and cause of the accusation; to be confronted with the witnesses against him; to have compulsory process for obtaining witnesses in his favor, and to have the assistance of counsel for his defense.

Amendment VII

In suits at common law, where the value in controversy shall exceed twenty dollars, the right of trial by jury shall be preserved, and no fact tried by a jury, shall be otherwise reexamined in any court of the United States, than according to the rules of the common law.

Amendment VIII

Excessive bail shall not be required, nor excessive fines imposed, nor cruel and unusual punishments inflicted.

Amendment IX

The enumeration in the Constitution, of certain rights, shall not be construed to deny or disparage others retained by the people.

Amendment X

The powers not delegated to the United States by the Constitution, nor prohibited by it to the states, are reserved to the states respectively, or to the people.

CHAPTER THREE
Fighting for freedom

"On a Tuesday morning, America went from a feeling of security to one of vulnerability, from peace to war, from a time of calm to a great and noble cause. We are called to defend liberty against tyranny and terror."

–President George W. Bush,

June 14, 2002

We are at war. Make no mistake about that.

Our enemies may not come at us in uniformed, organized battalions. They may not lead charges in armored vehicles or swarm in great masses of fighter planes.

Yet they are out there, ready to attack us–out of envy, religious fanaticism, or misunderstanding of what we are about. It doesn't really matter. We as a nation are once again called on to protect the principles on which the country was built and flourished.

Just as we have in the past.

There came times, just as now, when we've had to say enough is enough and back up our beliefs with guns. And from these conflicts, lessons were learned.

The first test the young country faced came some three decades after the Revolution in the War of 1812. Today many Americans know this "forgotten war" only by the song about the battle of New Orleans ("In 1814, we took a little trip along with Colonel Jackson down the might Mississipp") or that the words to the national anthem were written after the British attack on Fort McHenry in Baltimore.

American Colonel George Armistead asked that a flag be made so large that "the British would have no trouble seeing it from a distance." When the twenty-five hours of bombardment stopped and the flag was still flying, Francis Scott Key was inspired to write a poem that became the words of our anthem.

Oh, say can you see, by the dawn's early light,
What so proudly we hailed at the twilight's last gleaming?
Whose broad stripes and bright stars, through the perilous fight,
O'er the ramparts we watched, were so gallantly streaming?

And the rockets' red glare, the bombs bursting in air,
Gave proof through the night that our flag was still there.
O say, does that star-spangled banner yet wave
O'er the land of the free and the home of the brave?

On the shore, dimly seen through the mists of the deep,
Where the foe's haughty host in dread silence reposes,
What is that which the breeze, o'er the towering steep,
As it fitfully blows, now conceals, now discloses?
Now it catches the gleam of the morning's first beam,
In full glory reflected now shines on the stream:
'Tis the star-spangled banner! O long may it wave
O'er the land of the free and the home of the brave.

And where is that band who so vauntingly swore
That the havoc of war and the battle's confusion
A home and a country should leave us no more?
Their blood has wiped out their foul footstep's pollution.
No refuge could save the hireling and slave
From the terror of flight, or the gloom of the grave:
And the star-spangled banner in triumph doth wave
O'er the land of the free and the home of the brave.

The causes of the war? Sovereignty and trade. In the post-Revolution days, the United States had relied on diplomacy in dealing with Great Britain, not an easy task when England was the world's leading naval power (and didn't totally accept that it had lost its colonies).

As such a power, when England said it was going to board American ships looking for deserters from its navy, there wasn't much the U.S. could do about it. As a sovereign nation, our ships were our territory. But with only sixteen vessels in our navy, it was hard getting that point across.

Then, as part of its belligerent pas de deux with Napoleon, England proclaimed that no trading ship could enter European ports without first stopping in a British port and paying a fee. For the United States, this was too déjà vu from Colonial days.

Although the war was entered with some optimism, it was ill conceived. Our military preparedness was next to nonexistent with an army of a mere six thousand troops. The scope of the conflict was too vast. Canada was viewed as supporting Native Americans, who were opposing westward expansion. Invade Canada, cried one faction. It prevailed, and so the war was spread out and difficult to fight.

Both sides had victories. Both defeats. For the U.S., the most ignominious was the burning of the White House. First lady Dolly Madison, however, showed the American spunk by grabbing what she could before fleeing, including Gilbert Stuart's life-size portrait of George Washington, which had to be torn from its frame.

In the end–a draw. For the United States, the War of 1812 had its upside. Secretary of War John Calhoun made the case that to survive, the country could not depend on state militias–some well trained, others completely disorganized–to defend it. Nor could soldiers be asked to fight without adequate supplies, from blankets to bullets. In short, the United States needed a standing army, which it got.

The war also brought a renewed sense of patriotism and unity. The far-flung states with their regional differences and interests realized that they needed to stand together to survive.

* * *

Unfortunately for the 600,000 who died in the Civil War, lessons are forgotten. The differences between the states festered over the decades following the War of 1812. The South staunchly believed its agrarian, rural way of life–supported by slave labor–was a better and purer form of society. The North had become industrialized and commercial with free labor.

And there were increasingly loud voices coming from above the Mason-Dixon that condemned slavery as being immoral and contrary to the constitution and what the country had been founded on.

As often happens when emotions and stakes are high, reason can take a free fall down the rabbit hole into Wonderland. Southerners shouted back that a component of liberty–promised by the Founding Fathers–is the protection of private property. And by golly, slaves were private property. Why shouldn't someone be allowed to take his private property into the new territories and states out west?

And so the argument continued until Abraham Lincoln was elected president on a platform calling for the banning of slavery in the territories. The South had lost its hold on the federal government and feared being dominated by the North. It again fell back on defining "liberty." Liberty meant self-government. It was, therefore, the right of the South to secede from the union and establish its own government, just as the colonies had done in the Revolution.

Northern leaders had a different take on the subject. Having seen other republics collapse–most notably France, which had gone through two–they argued that a constitutional republic must be ruled by the majority. And just because someone gets elected president that one section of the country doesn't like, doesn't mean that faction can collect its marbles and call the whole thing off—which is in essence what the South did when it seceded.

Liberty could only be preserved if the union was preserved, the North contended.

From 1861 to 1865, the country was torn by the 10,000 skirmishes and battles that raged across the land, the last time battles were fought on the continental United States–until September 11, 2001. And in the end, the union prevailed and slavery was abolished by the Thirteenth Amendment.

There has been no challenge to the unity of the United States since. The Civil War stands as the severest test the nation ever faced to its fundamental structure, but it survived.

Our involvement in the wars of the twentieth century was in good part due to the world shrinking. Okay, so the number of miles on the Equator didn't change, but the time it took to get from one part of the globe to another did. Speed was the essence of the century. The speed of ships, then planes, then missiles increased exponentially.

We were drawn closer to our allies–and our enemies. The great oceans no longer were our impregnable moats. Thus we were forced into the great conflicts in Europe and the Far East.

World War I was a lethal brew of nationalism, economic competition, imperialism, and old grudges. And the United States wanted none of it.

With the outbreak of the war after the assassination of Archduke Ferdinand of Austria, the United States remained neutral–up to a point. We knew who were our friends and trading partners. Despite technically staying out of the war, we sold food, ammunition, and weapons to the Allies.

World War I was called the war to end all wars, partially because many could not fathom allowing such carnage again. In the Battle of Verdun alone, which lasted from February 21, 1916, to December 19, 1916, there were more than 700,000 dead, wounded, or missing.

The modern-age of warfare made its entry. Civilians would be bombed from the skies, thanks to zeppelins. Merchant ships were attacked by submarines from below the water. Armored vehicles took to the battlefield, and poisonous gas fouled the air.

But as much as many Americans wanted no part in the hostilities, the inevitable was in the offing.

There was outrage in the U.S. following the torpedoing of the British passenger ship Luisitania on May 7, 1915, by the Germans. One hundred and twenty-eight Americans lost their lives. Former President Teddy Roosevelt called for revenge while newspapers deemed the sinking "deliberate murder."

But it wasn't until 1917 that the United States gave up its neutrality. The government felt it had no choice after the British intercepted and deciphered the infamous Zimmerman telegram.

It was a message from the German foreign minister, Arthur Zimmerman, to his country's ambassador in Mexico. Dated January 19, Zimmerman said that as of February, Germany would begin unrestricted submarine warfare. If this resulted in the U.S. entry into the war, Germany was proposing an alliance with Mexico, after which financial support would be given for Mexico to retake lost territory in New Mexico, Texas, and Arizona.

Germany was in effect bringing the war to America's door, and America wasn't about to allow a home invasion. After three of our merchant ships were sunk by U-boats, the United States declared war on April 6, 1917, and President Woodrow Wilson sent the American Expeditionary Force under the command of General John Pershing "over there." And they didn't come back until it was "over over there."

More than 100,000 Americans died in World War I, a small number compared to the 1,400,000 French; 950,000 British; 1,700,000 Russians; 1,800,000 Germans; and 1,200,000 Austria-Hungarians. Still it was too high a number for Americans to stomach. They wanted to get back to the business of America–business.

And although Wilson campaigned hard to sell the notion of the League of Nations, the United States never joined. That left the league a toothless watchdog. And how were Americans to know that the $33 billion in reparations that Germany was ordered to pay would decimate its economy and leave it vulnerable to the insanity of Adolf Hitler?

Although it would take another world war for the lesson to be driven home, what was to be learned from World War I was that while we need to stand firm against tyranny, be it Hitler or Hussein, we must also have a just peace.

* * *

World War I, the war to end all wars? Not by a long shot, it was only the prelude to the largest conflict ever witnessed in the history of mankind–World War II.

By the time that war ended in 1945, 61 countries were involved. More than one-and-a-half billion people were involved—that was three-quarters of the world's population. More than 110 million served in the various armed forces. And the cost in terms of dollars and cents? More than one trillion dollars. It's estimated that some twenty-five million military personnel and 30 million civilians died—figures that do not include the six million killed in the Holocaust.

This was a war that came right through our door when the Japanese attacked Pearl Harbor on December 7, 1941. Until then President Franklin Roosevelt had tiptoed on a fine line of neutrality. But after that day of infamy, as Vice President Henry A. Wallace said, it was "a fight between a free world and a slave world."

With the invasion of Poland in September 1939, Hitler swept across the face of Europe. Denmark, Norway, France, Belgium, Luxembourg, the Netherlands, all fell with alarming speed. And Hitler promised, "Where Napoleon failed, I shall succeed. I shall land on the shores of Britain."

Meanwhile FDR worried that a Nazi push in North Africa was the first step toward invading the American mainland. The Nazis would cross the Atlantic at the bulge of the African continent, blitzkrieg through South and Central Americas and into the U.S.

On the Pacific front, Japan racked up victory after victory as it took Hong Kong, the Philippines, Wake Island, and Burma.

The fighting would go on for another four years until May 7, 1945, when all German forces surrendered unconditionally and August 14, 1945, when Japan capitulated.

The mettle of Americans, on the home front and the battlefront, was tested to the extreme, and they came out stronger than ever. Now the country was faced with the responsibility of being a superpower with nuclear capabilities, a responsibility that would only increase over the last half of the twentieth century.

The United States would stand up to aggression in Korea.

It would wage a Cold War with the Soviet Union.

It would get bogged down in Vietnam.

Under the leadership of Ronald Reagan, it would see the Berlin Wall come down and the Russian communist regime collapse.

And when Iraqi dictator Saddam Hussein thought he could get away with invading Kuwait, President George Herbert Walker Bush used diplomacy to forge a coalition then unleashed the power of the American armed forces and its allies on the aggressor.

Operation Desert Storm lasted from January 16 to February 28, 1991. As Lieutenant General Tom Kelly said, "Iraq went from the fourth-largest army in the world to the second-largest army in Iraq in 100 hours." While the U.S. suffered 148 killed in action, it is estimated that more than 100,000 Iraqi soldiers were killed and 300,000 wounded. In retrospect, the only thing that marred the coalition victory was that Saddam Hussein remained in power.

Then on September 11, 2001, America itself became a battleground. It was on that day that hijackers took control of four airliners and used three of them as missiles of destruction to attack symbols of the nation's might—the twin towers of the World Trade Center and the Pentagon. Only by the resolve and heroism of passengers on the fourth plane was the White House spared.

In a speech at West Point in June 2002, President George W. Bush reminded the graduating class that "America was attacked by a ruthless and resourceful enemy.... This war will take many turns we cannot predict. Yet I am certain of this, wherever we carry it, the American flag will stand not only for our power, but for freedom. Our nation's cause has always been larger than our nation's defense. We fight, as we always fight, for a just peace—a peace that favors human liberty. We will defend the peace against threats from terrorists and tyrants. We will preserve the peace by building good relations among the great powers. And we will extend the peace by encouraging free and open societies on every continent."

And that is something the Founding Fathers would applaud.

* * *

The Emancipation Proclamation

Whereas on the 22nd day of September, A.D. 1862, a proclamation was issued by the President of the United States, containing, among other things, the following, to wit:

"That on the 1st day of January, A.D. 1863, all persons held as slaves within any State or designated part of a State the people whereof shall then be in rebellion against the United States shall be then, thenceforward, and forever free; and the executive government of the United States, including the military and naval authority thereof, will recognize and maintain the freedom of such persons and will do no act or acts to repress such persons, or any of them, in any efforts they may make for their actual freedom.

"That the executive will on the 1st day of January aforesaid, by proclamation, designate the States and parts of States, if any, in which the people thereof, respectively, shall then be in rebellion against the United States; and the fact that any State or the people thereof shall on that day be in good faith represented in the Congress of the United States by members chosen thereto at elections wherein a majority of the qualified voters of such States shall have participated shall, in the absence of strong countervailing testimony, be deemed conclusive evidence that such State and the people thereof are not then in rebellion against the United States."

Now, therefore, I, Abraham Lincoln, President of the United States, by virtue of the power in me vested as Commander-In-Chief of the Army and Navy of the United States in time of actual armed rebellion against the authority and government of the United States, and as a fit and necessary war measure for supressing said rebellion, do, on this 1st day of January, A.D. 1863, and in accordance with my purpose so to do, publicly proclaimed for the full period of one hundred days from the first day above mentioned, order and designate as the States and parts of States wherein the people thereof, respectively, are this day in rebellion against the United States the following, to wit:

Arkansas, Texas, Louisiana (except the parishes of St. Bernard, Palquemines, Jefferson, St. John, St. Charles, St. James, Ascension,

Assumption, Terrebone, Lafourche, St. Mary, St. Martin, and Orleans, including the city of New Orleans), Mississippi, Alabama, Florida, Georgia, South Carolina, North Carolina, and Virginia (except the forty-eight counties designated as West Virginia, and also the counties of Berkeley, Accomac, Morthhampton, Elizabeth City, York, Princess Anne, and Norfolk, including the cities of Norfolk and Portsmouth), and which excepted parts are for the present left precisely as if this proclamation were not issued.

And by virtue of the power and for the purpose aforesaid, I do order and declare that all persons held as slaves within said designated States and parts of States are, and henceforward shall be, free; and that the Executive Government of the United States, including the military and naval authorities thereof, will recognize and maintain the freedom of said persons.

And I hereby enjoin upon the people so declared to be free to abstain from all violence, unless in necessary self-defence; and I recommend to them that, in all case when allowed, they labor faithfully for reasonable wages.

And I further declare and make known that such persons of suitable condition will be received into the armed service of the United States to garrison forts, positions, stations, and other places, and to man vessels of all sorts in said service.

And upon this act, sincerely believed to be an act of justice, warranted by the Constitution upon military necessity, I invoke the considerate judgment of mankind and the gracious favor of Almighty God.

–Abraham Lincoln, 1862

The Gettysburg Address, 1863

Fourscore and seven years ago our fathers brought forth on this continent a new nation, conceived in liberty and dedicated to the proposition that all men are created equal.

Now we are engaged in a great civil war, testing whether that nation or any nation so conceived and so dedicated can long endure.

We are met on a great battle field of that war. We have come to dedicate a portion of that field, as a final resting-place for those who here gave their lives that that nation might live. It is altogether fitting and proper that we should do this.

But, in a larger sense, we can not dedicate—we can not consecrate—we can not hallow—this ground. The brave men, living and dead, who struggled here, have consecrated it, far above our poor power to add or detract. The world will little note, nor long remember, what we say here, but it can never forget what they did here. It is for us the living, rather, to be dedicated here to the unfinished work which they who fought here have thus far so nobly advanced. It is rather for us to be here dedicated to the great task remaining before us—that from these honored dead we take increased devotion to that cause for which they gave the last full measure of devotion—that we here highly resolve that these dead shall not have died in vain—that this nation, under God, shall have a new birth of freedom—and that government of the people, by the people, for the people, shall not perish from the earth.

FDR's address to Congress after the attack on Pearl Harbor

To the Congress of the United States:

Yesterday, December 7, 1941—a date which will live in infamy—the United States of America was suddenly and deliberately attacked by naval and air forces of the empire of Japan.

The United States was at peace with that nation and, at the solicitation of Japan, was still in conversation with the government and its emperor looking toward the maintenance of peace in the Pacific.

Indeed, one hour after Japanese air squadrons had commenced bombing in Oahu, the Japanese ambassador to the United States and his colleagues delivered to the secretary of state a formal reply to a recent American message. While this reply stated that it seemed useless to continue the existing diplomatic negotiations, it contained no threat or hint of war or armed attack.

It will be recorded that the distance of Hawaii from Japan makes it obvious that the attack was deliberately planned many days or even weeks ago. During the intervening time, the Japanese government has deliberately sought to deceive the United States by false statements and expressions of hope for continued peace.

The attack yesterday on the Hawaiian Islands has caused severe damage to American naval and military forces. Very many American lives have been lost. In addition, American ships have been reported torpedoed on the high seas between San Francisco and Honolulu.

Yesterday, the Japanese government also launched an attack against Malaya.

Last night, Japanese forces attacked Hong Kong.

Last night, Japanese forces attacked Guam.

Last night, Japanese forces attacked the Philippine Islands.

Last night, the Japanese attacked Wake Island.

This morning, the Japanese attacked Midway Island.

Japan has, therefore, undertaken a surprise offensive extending throughout the Pacific area. The facts of yesterday speak for themselves. The people of the United States have already formed their opinions and well understand the implications to the very life and safety of our nation.

As commander in chief of the army and navy, I have directed that all measures be taken for our defense.

Always will we remember the character of the onslaught against us.

No matter how long it may take us to overcome this premeditated invasion, the American people in their righteous might will win through to absolute victory.

I believe I interpret the will of the Congress and of the people when I assert that we will not only defend ourselves to the uttermost, but will make very certain that this form of treachery shall never endanger us again.

Hostilities exist. There is no blinking at the fact that our people, our territory and our interests are in grave danger.

With confidence in our armed forces—with the unbounding determination of our people—we will gain the inevitable triumph—so help us God.

I ask that the Congress declare that since the unprovoked and dastardly attack by Japan on Sunday, December 7, a state of war has existed between the United States and the Japanese empire.

* * *

Ronald Reagan's speech at the Brandenburg Gate in Berlin, June 12, 1987, marked the beginning of the end of the hard-fought Cold War.

Twenty-four years ago, President John F. Kennedy visited Berlin, speaking to the people of this city and the world at the City Hall. Well, since then two other presidents have come, each in his turn, to Berlin. And today, I, myself, make my second visit to your city.

We come to Berlin, we American presidents, because it's our duty to speak, in this place, of freedom. But I must confess, we're drawn here by other things as well: by the feeling of history in this city, more than five hundred years older than our own nation; by the beauty of the Grunewald and the Tiergarten; most of all, by your courage and determination.

Perhaps the composer Paul Lincke understood something about American presidents. You see, like so many presidents before me, I come here today because wherever I go, whatever I do: Ich hab noch einen Koffer in Berlin.

Our gathering today is being broadcast throughout Western Europe and North America. I understand that it is being seen and heard as well in the East. To those listening in East Berlin, a special word: Although I cannot be with you, I address my remarks to you just as surely as to those standing here before me. For I join you, as I join your fellow countrymen in the West, in this firm, this unalterable belief: Es gibt nur ein Berlin.

43

Behind me stands a wall that encircles the free sectors of this city, part of a vast system of barriers that divides the entire continent of Europe. From the Baltic, south, those barriers cut across Germany in a gash of barbed wire, concrete, dog runs, and guard towers. Farther south, there may be no visible, no obvious wall. But there remain armed guards and checkpoints all the same—still a restriction on the right to travel, still an instrument to impose upon ordinary men and women the will of a totalitarian state. Yet it is here in Berlin where the wall emerges most clearly; here, cutting across your city, where the news photo and the television screen have imprinted this brutal division of a continent upon the mind of the world. Standing before the Brandenburg Gate, every man is a German, separated from his fellow men. Every man is a Berliner, forced to look upon a scar.

President von Weizsacker has said, "The German question is open as long as the Brandenburg Gate is closed." Today I say: As long as the gate is closed, as long as this scar of a wall is permitted to stand, it is not the German question alone that remains open, but the question of freedom for all mankind. Yet I do not come here to lament. For I find in Berlin a message of hope, even in the shadow of this wall, a message of triumph.

In this season of spring in 1945, the people of Berlin emerged from their air-raid shelters to find devastation. Thousands of miles away, the people of the United States reached out to help. And in 1947 Secretary of State . . . George Marshall announced the creation of what would become known as the Marshall Plan. Speaking precisely forty years ago this month, he said, "Our policy is directed not against any country or doctrine, but against hunger, poverty, desperation, and chaos."

In the Reichstag a few moments ago, I saw a display commemorating this fortieth anniversary of the Marshall Plan. I was struck by the sign on a burnt-out, gutted structure that was being rebuilt. I understand that Berliners of my own generation can remember seeing signs like it dotted throughout the western sectors of the city. The sign read simply: "The Marshall Plan is helping here to strengthen the free world." A strong, free world in the West, that dream became real. Japan rose from ruin to become an economic giant. Italy, France,

Belgium—virtually every nation in Western Europe saw political and economic rebirth; the European Community was founded.

In West Germany and here in Berlin, there took place an economic miracle, the Wirtschaftswunder. Adenauer, Erhard, Reuter, and other leaders understood the practical importance of liberty—that just as truth can flourish only when the journalist is given freedom of speech, so prosperity can come about only when the farmer and businessman enjoy economic freedom. The German leaders reduced tariffs, expanded free trade, lowered taxes. From 1950 to 1960 alone, the standard of living in West Germany and Berlin doubled.

Where four decades ago there was rubble, today in West Berlin there is the greatest industrial output of any city in Germany—busy office blocks, fine homes and apartments, proud avenues, and the spreading lawns of parkland. Where a city's culture seemed to have been destroyed, today there are two great universities, orchestras and an opera, countless theaters, and museums. Where there was want, today there's abundance—food, clothing, automobiles—the wonderful goods of the Ku'damm. From devastation, from utter ruin, you Berliners have, in freedom, rebuilt a city that once again ranks as one of the greatest on earth. The Soviets may have had other plans. But my friends, there were a few things the Soviets didn't count on—Berliner Herz, Berliner Humor, ja, and Berliner Schnauze. [Berliner heart, Berliner humor, yes, and a Berliner Schnauze.]

In the 1950s, Khrushchev predicted, "We will bury you." But in the West today, we see a free world that has achieved a level of prosperity and well being unprecedented in all human history. In the Communist world, we see failure, technological backwardness, declining standards of health, even want of the most basic kind—too little food. Even today, the Soviet Union still cannot feed itself. After these four decades, then, there stands before the entire world one great and inescapable conclusion: Freedom leads to prosperity. Freedom replaces the ancient hatreds among the nations with comity and peace. Freedom is the victor.

And now the Soviets themselves may, in a limited way, becoming to understand the importance of freedom. We hear much from Moscow

45

about a new policy of reform and openness. Some political prisoners have been released. Certain foreign news broadcasts are no longer being jammed. Some economic enterprises have been permitted to operate with greater freedom from state control.

Are these the beginnings of profound changes in the Soviet state? Or are they token gestures, intended to raise false hopes in the West, or to strengthen the Soviet system without changing it? We welcome change and openness; for we believe that freedom and security go together, that the advance of human liberty can only strengthen the cause of world peace. There is one sign the Soviets can make that would be unmistakable, that would advance dramatically the cause of freedom and peace.

General Secretary Gorbachev, if you seek peace, if you seek prosperity for the Soviet Union and Eastern Europe, if you seek liberalization: Come here to this gate! Mr. Gorbachev, open this gate! Mr. Gorbachev, tear down this wall!

I understand the fear of war and the pain of division that afflict this continent—and I pledge to you my country's efforts to help overcome these burdens. To be sure, we in the West must resist Soviet expansion. So we must maintain defenses of unassailable strength. Yet we seek peace; so we must strive to reduce arms on both sides.

Beginning ten years ago, the Soviets challenged the Western alliance with a grave new threat, hundreds of new and more deadly SS-20 nuclear missiles, capable of striking every capital in Europe. The Western alliance responded by committing itself to a counterdeployment unless the Soviets agreed to negotiate a better solution; namely, the elimination of such weapons on both sides. For many months, the Soviets refused to bargain in earnestness. As the alliance, in turn, prepared to go forward with its counterdeployment, there were difficult days—days of protests like those during my 1982 visit to this city—and the Soviets later walked away from the table.

But through it all, the alliance held firm. And I invite those who protested then—I invite those who protest today—to mark this fact: Because we remained strong, the Soviets came back to the table. And because we remained strong, today we have within reach the possibility, not merely of limiting the growth of arms, but of eliminating, for the first time, an entire class of nuclear weapons from the face of the earth.

As I speak NATO ministers are meeting in Iceland to review the progress of our proposals for eliminating these weapons. At the talks in Geneva, we have also proposed deep cuts in strategic offensive weapons. And the Western allies have likewise made far-reaching proposals to reduce the danger of conventional war and to place a total ban on chemical weapons.

While we pursue these arms reductions, I pledge to you that we will maintain the capacity to deter Soviet aggression at any level at which it might occur. And in cooperation with many of our allies, the United States is pursuing the Strategic Defense Initiative—research to base deterrence not on the threat of offensive retaliation, but on defenses that truly defend; on systems, in short, that will not target populations, but shield them. By these means we seek to increase the safety of Europe and all the world. But we must remember a crucial fact: East and West do not mistrust each other because we are armed; we are armed because we mistrust each other. And our differences are not about weapons, but about liberty. When President Kennedy spoke at the City Hall those twenty-four years ago, freedom was encircled, Berlin was under siege. And today, despite all the pressures upon this city, Berlin stands secure in its liberty. And freedom itself is transforming the globe.

In the Philippines, in South and Central America, democracy has been given a rebirth. Throughout the Pacific, free markets are working miracle after miracle of economic growth. In the industrialized nations, a technological revolution is taking place—a revolution marked by rapid, dramatic advances in computers and telecommunications. In Europe, only one nation and those it controls refuse to join the community of freedom. Yet in this age of redoubled economic growth, of information and innovation, the Soviet Union faces a choice: It must make fundamental changes, or it will become obsolete.

Today thus represents a moment of hope. We in the West stand ready to cooperate with the East to promote true openness, to break down barriers that separate people, to create a safe, freer world. And surely there is no better place than Berlin, the meeting place of East and West, to make a start. Free people of Berlin: Today, as in the past, the United States stands for the strict observance and full implementation of all parts of the Four Power Agreement of 1971. Let us use this occasion, the 750th anniversary of this city, to usher in a new era, to seek a still fuller, richer life for the Berlin of the future. Together, let us maintain and develop the ties between the Federal Republic and the Western sectors of Berlin, which is permitted by the 1971 agreement.

And I invite Mr. Gorbachev: Let us work to bring the Eastern and Western parts of the city closer together, so that all the inhabitants of all Berlin can enjoy the benefits that come with life in one of the great cities of the world.

To open Berlin still further to all Europe, East and West, let us expand the vital air access to this city, finding ways of making commercial air service to Berlin more convenient, more comfortable, and more economical. We look to the day when West Berlin can become one of the chief aviation hubs in all central Europe.

With our French and British partners, the United States is prepared to help bring international meetings to Berlin. It would be only fitting for Berlin to serve as the site of United Nations meetings, or world conferences on human rights and arms control or other issues that call for international cooperation.

There is no better way to establish hope for the future than to enlighten young minds, and we would be honored to sponsor summer youth exchanges, cultural events, and other programs for young Berliners from the East. Our French and British friends, I'm certain, will do the same. And it's my hope that an authority can be found in East Berlin to sponsor visits from young people of the Western sectors.

One final proposal, one close to my heart: Sport represents a source of enjoyment and ennoblement, and you may have noted that the Republic of Korea–South Korea–has offered to permit certain events of the 1988 Olympics to take place in the North. International sports competitions of all kinds could take place in both parts of this city. And what better way to demonstrate to the world the openness of this city than to offer in some future year to hold the Olympic games here in Berlin, East and West?

In these four decades, as I have said, you Berliners have built a great city. You've done so in spite of threats—the Soviet attempts to impose the East-mark, the blockade. Today the city thrives in spite of the challenges implicit in the very presence of this wall. What keeps you here? Certainly there's a great deal to be said for your fortitude, for your defiant courage. But I believe there's something deeper, something that involves Berlin's whole look and feel and way of life—not mere sentiment. No one could live long in Berlin without being completely disabused of illusions. Something instead, that has seen the difficulties of life in Berlin, but chose to accept them, that continues to build this good and proud city in contrast to a surrounding totalitarian presence that refuses to release human energies or aspirations. Something that speaks with a powerful voice of affirmation, that says yes to this city, yes to the future, yes to freedom. In a word, I would submit that what keeps you in Berlin is love—love both profound and abiding.

Perhaps this gets to the root of the matter, to the most fundamental distinction of all between East and West. The totalitarian world produces backwardness because it does such violence to the spirit, thwarting the human impulse to create, to enjoy, to worship. The totalitarian world finds even symbols of love and of worship an affront. Years ago, before the East Germans began rebuilding their churches, they erected a secular structure: the television tower at Alexander Platz. Virtually ever since, the authorities have been working to correct what they view as the tower's one major flaw, treating the glass sphere at the top with paints and chemicals of every kind. Yet even today when the sun strikes that sphere—that sphere that towers over all Berlin—the light makes the sign of the cross. There in Berlin, like the city itself, symbols of love, symbols of worship, cannot be suppressed.

As I looked out a moment ago from the Reichstag, that embodiment of German unity, I noticed words crudely spray-painted upon the wall, perhaps by a young Berliner: "This wall will fall. Beliefs become reality." Yes, across Europe, this wall will fall. For it cannot withstand *faith; it cannot withstand truth. The wall cannot withstand freedom.*

And I would like, before I close, to say one word. I have read, and I have been questioned since I've been here about certain demonstrations against my coming. And I would like to say just one thing, and to those who demonstrate so. I wonder if they have ever asked themselves that if they should have the kind of government they apparently seek, no one would ever be able to do what they're doing again.

Thank you and God bless you all.

* * *

It is ironic that a George, George Washington, was the man who gave us our freedom back in the eighteenth century. Now at the beginning of the twenty-first, our leader is another George, George W. Bush, who has been charged with having us maintain our freedoms and all of which we have gained since 1776.

Nine/eleven will not only go down with the same infamy that was struck us at Pearl Harbor in 1941, but will also be remembered as the first time our nation, our mainland, our way of life was struck with demolition of the Twin Towers and the strike at the Pentagon.

George W. Bush has said much since September 11, 2001, but this particular address to the nation, one year later, eloquently sums up the spirit of freedom that will live forever.

A long year has passed since enemies attacked our country. We've seen the images so many times they are seared on our souls, and remembering the horror, reliving the anguish, reimagining the terror, is hard—and painful.

For those who lost loved ones, it's been a year of sorrow, of empty places, of newborn children who will never know their fathers here on earth. For members of our military, it's been a year of sacrifice and service far from home. For all Americans, it has been a year of adjustment, of coming to terms with the difficult knowledge that our nation has determined enemies and that we are not invulnerable to their attacks.

Yet, in the events that have challenged us, we have also seen the character that will deliver us. We have seen the greatness of America in airline passengers who defied their hijackers and ran a plane into the ground to spare the lives of others. We've seen the greatness of America in rescuers who rushed up flights of stairs toward peril. And we continue to see the greatness of America in the care and compassion our citizens show to each other.

September 11, 2001, will always be a fixed point in the life of America. The loss of so many lives left us to examine our own. Each of us was reminded that we are here only for a time, and these counted days should be filled with things that last and matter: love for our families, love for our neighbors, and for our country; gratitude for life and to the Giver of life.

We resolved a year ago to honor every last person lost. We owe them remembrance, and we owe them more. We owe them, and their children, and our own, the most enduring monument we can build: a world of liberty and security made possible by the way America leads and by the way Americans lead our lives.

The attack on our nation was also attack on the ideals that make us a nation. Our deepest national conviction is that every life is precious, because every life is the gift of a Creator who intended us to live in liberty and equality. More than anything else, this separates us from the enemy we fight. We value every life; our enemies value none—not even the innocent, not even their own. And we seek the freedom and opportunity that give meaning and value to life.

There is a line in our time, and in every time, between those who believe all men are created equal and those who believe that some men and women and children are expendable in the pursuit of power. There is a line in our time, and in every time, between the defenders of human liberty and those who seek to master the minds and souls of others. Our generation has now heard history's call, and we will answer it.

America has entered a great struggle that tests our strength and

51

even more our resolve. Our nation is patient and steadfast. We con-
tinue to pursue the terrorists in cities and camps and caves across the
earth. We are joined by a great coalition of nations to rid the world of
terror. And we will not allow any terrorist or tyrant to threaten civi-
lization with weapons of mass murder. Now and in the future,
Americans will live as free people, not in fear, and never at the mercy
of any foreign plot or power.

This nation has defeated tyrants and liberated death camps, raised
this lamp of liberty to every captive land. We have no intention of
ignoring or appeasing history's latest gang of fanatics trying to murder
their way to power. They are discovering, as others before them, the
resolve of a great country and a great democracy. In the ruins of two
towers, under a flag unfurled at the Pentagon, at the funerals of the
lost, we have made a sacred promise to ourselves and to the world: We
will not relent until justice is done and our nation is secure. What our
enemies have begun, we will finish.

I believe there is a reason that history has matched this nation
with this time. America strives to be tolerant and just. We respect the
faith of Islam, even as we fight those whose actions defile that faith. We
fight, not to impose our will, but to defend ourselves and extend the
blessings of freedom.

We cannot know all that lies ahead. Yet, we do know that God
had placed us together in this moment, to grieve together, to stand
together, to serve each other and our country. And the duty we have
been given—defending America and our freedom—is also a privilege we
share.

We're prepared for this journey. And our prayer tonight is that
God will see us through and keep us worthy.

Tomorrow is September the twelfth. A milestone is passed, and a
mission goes on. Be confident. Our country is strong. And our cause is
even larger than our country. Ours is the cause of human dignity; free-
dom guided by conscience and guarded by peace. This ideal of America
is the hope of all mankind. That hope drew millions to this harbor.
That hope still lights our way. And the light shines in the darkness.

And the darkness will not overcome it.

    May God bless America.

* * *

And so it has been since the Revolution's battles for our freedom to this very day's fight to maintain our freedom and way of life–we shall persevere.

PART II

We are all immigrants

CHAPTER FOUR
The magnet of liberty

Sixty-seven days.

Sixty-seven days of monstrous North Atlantic storms that threatened to swallow up the tiny vessel.

Sixty-seven days of roiling and rolling in cramped, wet quarters that reeked of seasickness. "Many fierce winds with which the ship was shrewdly shaken," was how leader William Bradford put it.

But when given the chance to turn back, the passengers on the battered ship opted to push westward even though ahead of them was uncertainty and hardship.

Finally on a bleak November day, the cry of "land ho" was heard, and the Pilgrims of the *Mayflower*, arrived on the shores of a promised land.

The landscape may have been desolate and forbidding, but these seventy adults, thirty-two children, and two dogs were willing to risk all for the chance at a better life, just as the millions upon millions of immigrants who followed them were also willing to do. They came–and still come–searching for hope and freedom.

We are a nation of immigrants. Make no mistake about that.

Shake any American's genealogical tree, and an immigrant falls out. At one point or another, we all came from someplace else. (Admittedly, Native Americans have the longest claim on living here, but even their ancestors either came across the Bering Sea or jumped from Africa to South America when the continents were closer.)

There are some, because the first in their family arrived in the seventeenth or eighteenth century, who would lead you to believe they have some sort of exclusivity on being "American." Nonsense, they are as much immigrants as those whose mothers and fathers came over in steerage from Europe during the nineteenth century or by jetliner from Asia in the twentieth.

We are all immigrants.

Of course, over the decades as times have changed, there have been changes in our national perception of whom and how many we can take in.

During Colonial times, everyone, almost without exception, was welcomed. We had such a vast and beckoning land, citizens were needed to populate it. People were willing to take the risks and face the dangers across the Atlantic because of the opportunities that were offered.

If you grew up in the United States, the phrase "land of opportunity" is a very familiar one. But it was more than a phrase to those who came to our shores; it spelled hope and the possibility for a better future.

"The only encouragement we hold out to strangers are a good climate, fertile soil, wholesome air and water, plenty of provisions, good pay for labor, kind neighbors, good laws, a free government, and a hearty welcome." Benjamin Franklin said that, and millions listened.

Whether life was wonderful and rosy for newcomers as Franklin suggested, was not the point. The point was that it could be. Work hard, and you could succeed.

Life might be hard here, but for those fleeing persecution and starvation, it held a promise of better days.

* * *

One of the first enormous swells of migration came during the Great Hunger in Ireland. With blight ruining potato crop after potato crop, it's believed that one million people died from starvation between 1845 and 1855. Two million fled the famine, many suffering incredible hardships and degradations on their journey to the United States.

Ships fit to carry 300 passengers were crammed with 500. The rations of sea biscuits were moldy and tough. Water was doled out sparingly, if at all.

People were supposed to get at least thirty-three inches of bunk space. That was often cut in half, still leaving many with no place to sleep. In steerage, there were no portholes or lights. The air quickly turned stagnant with sweat and urine. In these miserable conditions, there was always the danger of disease.

One immigrant wrote of reaching the St. Lawrence River. "I saw a shapeless heap move past our ship on the outgoing tide. Presently there was another and another. Craning my head over the bulwark, I watched. Another came and it caught in our cable and before the swish of the current washed it clear, I caught a glimpse of a white face. I understood it all. The ship ahead of us had emigrants and they were throwing overboard their dead."

The magnet of America was enough to keep the Irish coming.

They wanted to live the American Dream, food for the family, jobs, schooling for the children, and chance for a better life for themselves and a still-better one for their children and grandchildren.

The oppression of war also sent refugees scurrying to sanctuary in America. In the mid-nineteenth century, many fled from Germany after the Revolution of 1848 broke out against the Prussians. One young German, Carl Schurz, was able to escape under harrowing circumstances through a town sewer. After reaching safety in Alsace, he realized he couldn't return to his home, so where could he go to live a full and worthwhile life? "'To America,' I said to myself. 'The ideals of which I have dreamed and for which I have fought, I shall find there. . . . It is a new world, a free world, a world of great ideas and aims. In that world there is perhaps for me a new home."

Schurz went on to become an adamant abolitionist, a general in the Union army, and the first German-American to serve in the Senate.

He wrote of his first day in Congress. "Little more than sixteen years had elapsed since I had landed on these shores, a homeless waif, saved from the wreck of a revolutionary movement in Europe. Then I was enfolded in the generous hospitality of the American people, opening to me as freely as to its own children the great opportunities of the new world. And here I was now a member of the highest lawmaking body of the greatest of republics."

And so they came, from Germany, the United Kingdom, and Ireland. They were followed by Scandinavians, Chinese, and South Americans. And then southern and eastern Europeans.

In a forty-year span, from 1880 to 1920, four million Italians came to the U.S. The history of Italy was one of feuding states and feudalism. What you could accomplish in life was based on birth. Who could own land depended on who your father and his father and his father were. Poverty for most Italians was their past, present, and future.

No wonder Italian families forsook the little they had to reach America. It's true that on their arrival, they were met by disappointment. The jobs available to them were hard labor—working in coal mines, hoisting beams for new buildings, digging ditches.

However, there was the promise that in this country perseverance would bring rewards. Saving their money, Italians opened fruit stores, small groceries, flower shops. And things got better.

Edward Corsi, who later became commissioner of immigration at Ellis Island, remembered sailing into New York harbor with his family.

"Mothers and fathers lifted up the babies so that they, too, could see, off to the left, the Statue of Liberty.

"I looked at that statue with a sense of bewilderment, half doubting its reality. Looming shadowy through the mist, it brought silence to the decks [of the ship]. This symbol of America inspired awe in the hopeful immigrants."

And when the ship docked, Corsi and his family disembarked at Ellis Island, what journalist and social reformer Jacob Riis called "the nation's gateway to the promised land."

The United States remained the "promised land" throughout the crises and conflicts of the twentieth century. Where else would the displaced people of World War I go? We saw a 300-percent increase of immigrants from just 1919 to 1920.

After World War II, we again opened our door to those with no homes and little hope. In 1956, after the armed uprising in Hungary, challenging the Soviet-backed regime, where would those fleeing the repressions and reprisals go? The insurrection only lasted from October 23 to November 14. But when it was over, 35,000 were put on trial, 25,000 to 26,000 were jailed, and scores executed. It was not until 1963 that the retaliations ended with a general amnesty. Thirty-two thousand Hungarians managed to find refuge in America.

After Fidel Castro's takeover of Cuba in 1959, opponents to his regime turned to us.

And still they come.

Wherever there is hardship and oppression, those yearning to breathe free seek a new life and the chance to succeed in the United States.

Here thoughts and new ideas are encouraged. Dissent is not crushed under the weight of weapons and tanks. Enterprise is rewarded. A utopia? No, but try and tell that to some of those who risked everything to reach here.

They would embrace and cherish the four freedoms Franklin Delano Roosevelt outlined in his 1941 state of the union address.

On the brink of our entering World War II, FDR sought to remind Americans what we had to fight to preserve.

He began by his speech to the seventy-seventh Congress by saying, "I address you . . . at a moment unprecedented in the history of the union. I use the word 'unprecedented' because at no previous time has American security been as seriously threatened from without as it is today.

"Since the permanent formation of our government under the Constitution in 1789, most of the periods of crisis in our history have related to our domestic affairs. And, fortunately, only one of these–the four year war between the states–ever threatened our national unity. "Today, thank God, 130,000,000 Americans in forty-eight states have forgotten points of the compass in our national unity."

He went on to spell out why the country needed to be prepared to go to war and concluded with "in the future days which we seek to make secure, we look forward to a world founded upon four essential human freedoms. "The first is freedom of speech and expression–everywhere in the world. The second is freedom of every person to worship God in his own way–everywhere in the world. The third is freedom from want, which, translated into world terms, means economic understandings which will secure to every nation a healthy peacetime life for its inhabitants–everywhere in the world. The fourth is freedom from fear, which, translated into world terms, means a worldwide reduction of armaments to such a point and in such a thorough fashion that no nation will be in a position to commit an act of physical aggression against any neighbor–everywhere in the world."

* * *

"Everywhere in the world" may never come to pass, which is why the Carl Schurzes and Edward Corsis, past, present, and future, will risk their possessions, lives and the lives of their children to be Americans.

Emma Lazarus' paean to the Statue of Liberty, 1883

"The New Colossus"

Not like the brazen giant of Greek fame
With conquering limbs astride from land to land;
Here at our sea-washed, sunset gates shall stand
A mighty woman with a torch, whose flame
Is the imprisoned lightning, and her name
Mother of Exiles. From her beacon-hand
Glows world-wide welcome; her mild eyes command
The air-bridged harbor that twin cities frame,
"Keep, ancient lands, your storied pomp!" cries she
With silent lips. "Give me your tired, your poor,
Your huddled masses yearning to breathe free,
The wretched refuse of your teeming shore,
Send these, the homeless, tempest-tossed to me,
I lift my lamp beside the golden door!"

CHAPTER FIVE
Faces of the nation

From Puritans on the *Mayflower* through today, immigrants have graced our shores and added to the strength and prosperity of the nation.

Here are a few, random portraits of first- and second-generation immigrants, past and present, who so contributed to our well-being.

John Paul Jones
Father of American navy

The man who became a Revolutionary War naval hero because of his audacious exploits, was born July 6, 1747, to a Scottish gardener,

He took to the sea at age twelve as an apprentice, with his first voyage taking him to Virginia. By age twenty-one, Jones had made captain. He plied the Caribbean waters in commercial ventures. But when a Continental navy was formed by the American colonies, in preparation of fighting for their independence, Jones asked to join. In December 1775, he was commissioned as first lieutenant rising quickly to captaincy.

His most famous battle of the Revolution came September 23, 1779, when his *Alliance* took on the *H.M.S. Serapis* in the North Sea.

The battle raged for three-and-a-half hours with more than half the Alliance crew killed, wounded, or severely burned. At one point, Jones was asked to surrender, to which he so famously replied, "I have not yet begun to fight."

In the end, it was the English who had to surrender.

* * *

Elizabeth Blackwell
First female physician in the United States

In the mid-nineteenth century, women did not attend medical colleges, much less become doctors. But that wasn't going to stop Elizabeth Blackwell, who emigrated from England at age thirteen in 1834.

A dying friend had urged her to become a doctor, and she was determined to do so despite first facing rejection from nineteen schools.

Then in 1847, almost by fluke, she was accepted by Geneva (now Hobart) Medical College. Two years later, she graduated at the top of her class, making her the first female physician in the country's history.

Blackwell's life was one of grit, determination, and perseverance–so much a part of the American character. After her father died penniless when she was a young woman, Blackwell taught school. Not finding the vocation challenging enough, she listened to her friend and took to the path of medicine.

Throughout her career, Blackwell met rejections and barriers from the established medical community. After graduating from Geneva, no American hospital would give her a residency. It was merely another obstacle. Blackwell went to work in a lowly position at a maternity hospital in Paris, where a mishap led to the loss of an eye. She wanted experience, and she would get it wherever she could and under whatever conditions she could. Finally, a British physician pulled strings, and Blackwell was admitted to the renowned St. Bartholomew's Hospital in London.

Back in the United States, she was met with more rejection, as no male doctor would join her in a practice. But the indomitable American spirit imbued this transplanted Englishwoman. She went into practice by herself, in Jersey City, and waited for patients.

The determination finally paid off when she, her sister (who followed her into medicine), and a third female doctor opened the New York Infirmary for Women and Children on Bleecker Street in New York City and later a medical school for women.

Blackwell forced open the barred door to the medical profession. At the time of her death in 1910, there were 7,399 females who were licensed physicians and surgeons. All because she wouldn't take no for an answer.

* * *

Joseph Goldberger
Pioneer medical researcher

Hungary, part of the Austro-Hungarian Empire, was a harsh homeland for sheepherders. Life was a struggle to survive, but that struggle became near insurmountable when a sickness swept through the flocks, killing most of them.

Faced with destitution, the parents of Joseph Goldberger, who was born in 1874, plunged toward hope. They abandoned the familiar, relatives and something so basic as native language, took their family of four children and emigrated from Hungary to what they were confident would be a better life. They immigrated to the United States.

As so many newcomers before and since did, they opened a small grocery store. They added three more children to the family and worked long, arduous hours to support them and give them the promise of a better life.

Joseph, after going through the New York public school system, entered the City College of New York with the idea of becoming an engineer. Luckily for victims of the horrendous disease, pellagra, Goldberger switched career paths after hearing a lecture by physiologist Dr. August Flint, Jr. The structure of a building was no longer what fascinated Goldberger. It was now the structure of the human body.

He transferred into the medical school. In 1899, after an unsatisfying stint in private practice, Goldberger joined the United States Marine Hospital Services. His job? An immigrant was now inspecting immigrants entering the United States for health problems.

But that was merely a way stop. Goldberger's epidemiological skills took him to Puerto Rico, Mexico, Louisiana, and Mississippi, where he fought yellow fever. He contracted the disease himself, as he would later dengue fever and typhus.

But it was finding the cause for pellagra that would overshadow all his other accomplishments.

Pellagra is a potentially fatal and loathsome disease that can be mistaken for leprosy. The widely held belief was pellagra was caused by germs. Goldberger rejected that hypothesis. Studying prison inmates, he noted those behind bars had the disease, but not the guards. If the cause was germs, that made no sense.

Goldberger was sure something lacking in the diet caused the disease.

He worked until his death to prove his theory. He even went so far as injecting himself, an assistant, his wife, and other volunteers with blood contaminated with pellagra. No one got the disease. That being the case, how could a germ be causing it?

His fierce contention that pellagra was a dietary disease would prove correct.

As Alan Kraut, professor of history, American University 1996 Stetten Museum Senior Visiting Fellow, sees it, "Heroes are few in science as in every field. However, the selfless devotion of Dr. Joseph Goldberger to relieving the suffering of those whose plague was born of poverty might well qualify him for the garland."

Today Goldberger may be a footnote in medical science, but he is definitely a strong stitch in the fabric of our immigrant history.

* * *

Thomas Alva Edison
Inventor extraordinaire

Who can say whether the spirit of invention would have overpowered Thomas Alva Edison had his parents decided to stay in Canada?

What is known is that quintessential American drive to achieve was certainly imbued in Edison. Born in 1847 in Milan, Ohio, Edison did not show early genius. When a teacher called him "addled," Edison's mother, Nancy, removed him from school and taught him at home. Even when he was young, Edison showed a marked interest in mechanics and chemistry.

At twelve, Edison became almost totally deaf. But he didn't allow that handicap to stand in the way of his life's work. In fact, he claimed it made it easier for him to concentrate.

And concentrate he did. He held 1,093 patents and invented hundreds of things that changed the very way we live. Phonograph. Incandescent light bulb. Motion picture camera. First electric motor. Wireless telegraphy. Giant rolling machine for crushing rock. Steel alkaline storage battery. The list goes on and on.

On top of all that, Edison formed and ran several successful businesses.

Thomas Alva Edison died at age eighty-four October 18, 1931, leaving an incredible mark on his country.

* * *

David Sarnoff
Communications pioneer

If you're looking for grit and determination, a story that even Horatio Alger could not have imagined, then look no further than David Sarnoff.

He was born in Russia to a poverty-stricken Jewish painter in 1891. When David was five, his father, Abraham Sarnoff, like so many other Russian Jews at the time, left his family in search of something better in the United States.

After four years, Abraham had scrounged enough savings performing menial jobs to send for his family. David's new home was a squalid fourth-story walk-up on the Lower East Side of New York City. The family was in such dire straits that the young boy took to the streets selling a Yiddish newspaper. If he sold fifty, he was paid a quarter. He got up each morning at 4 so that he would be the first on the street to establish his territory.

By the time he was fourteen, Sarnoff had the wherewithal to open a newspaper stand. He then taught himself the Morse code and got a job as a gofer for the Marconi Wireless Telegraph Company. Who would have guessed that was to change the course of American broadcasting?

By 1908, Sarnoff had risen to junior operator, and on April 14, 1912, was working when a message came in from ships at sea. "*S.S. Titanic* ran into iceberg, sinking fast." Sarnoff manned his post for seventy-two hours, relaying to the nation the horrendous news.

In these early days, the wireless was used primarily in shipping. But Sarnoff had the idea of making a "radio music box" that would bring entertainment into the homes of America. He continued to push the idea after General Electric took over Marconi's American operations and formed RCA.

He argued that to get people to buy the radio music box, there had to be programming that would make them want to tune in. And so it was that in 1921 Sarnoff got the Jack Dempsey-Georges Carpentier fight on the air, and the rest was history. Three years later, the box, dubbed the Radiola, had hit $83.5 million in sales.

Not satisfied with this success, Sarnoff created the National Broadcasting Company by bringing together hundreds of stations across the country.

Sarnoff also led in the development of television, becoming one of the most powerful men in the broadcast industry.

When he died in his sleep in 1971, the *New York Times* ran his obituary on page one, jumping to a full page inside. The obituary stated, "He was not an inventor, nor was he a scientist. But he was a man of astounding vision who was able to see with remarkable clarity the possibilities of harnessing the electron."

* * *

Dr. Antonia Coello Novello
First woman, first Hispanic U.S. surgeon general

The story of Dr. Antonia Coello Novello, the first woman and first Hispanic to ever hold the office of surgeon general of the U.S. Public Health Service, is one of overcoming debilitating adversity, setting a goal, and working to achieve it.

Antonia Coello was born August 23, 1944, in the small town of Fajardo in the U.S. territory of Puerto Rico.

As a child, Coello suffered from a digestive disease. She had to spend two weeks of every summer as a child in the hospital. The doctors and nurses so impressed her, she decided to go to medical school.

Her mother pushed her to excel in school, ensuring she had the best teachers available. Coello graduated high school when she was fifteen and entered the University of Puerto Rico.

Then, at 18, she had her first surgery to correct her intestinal disease. When she turned 20, she made her first visit to mainland United States for final surgery and treatment at the Mayo Clinic.

She worked to fulfill her childhood dream of becoming a doctor by going to the University of Puerto Rico's medical school. She interned at the University of Michigan's pediatric nephrology unit, treating children with kidney diseases.

In 1979 she began a long career of public service, joining the National Institutes of Health (NIH), developing a particular expertise in pediatric AIDS while at the NIH.

In 1989 President George Bush named her surgeon general, replacing her former boss, Dr. C. Everett Koop.

She later told the *Puerto Rico Herald*, "Being the first woman and minority surgeon general enables me to reach many individuals with my message of empowerment for women, children, and minorities."

Novello believes the time was certainly right for a woman and a minority to serve in that position. It was also an important time for someone with an expertise in the AIDS epidemic to have a voice in formulating public health policy.

"I truly believe that they needed someone who could show the American dream, all of those things together," she remembered in the 1994 *Herald* interview. "I think the time was right for someone who was kind of conservative, but with common sense. I think I was selected for all those things together. It was a package deal. Then I had to prove that it can be done."

Novello is currently the New York State health commissioner appointed by Gov. George Pataki in June 1999.

Novello believes in the American dream.

"The American dream continues because every time that I speak, somebody believes that they can be me," she has said.

* * *

Yo-Yo Ma
World-renowned cellist

Up at the top of the roster of immigrants who have contributed so greatly to the arts in America is Yo-Yo Ma.

This incredible virtuoso was born in Paris to Chinese parents. In 1959, at age four, Yo-Yo Ma took to studying the cello and gave his first public concert a year later.

Three years after that, the family arrived in the United States. After studying at Julliard, he attended Harvard University from 1972 to 1976. It was composer Leonard Bernstein who turned the attention of the nation on this elegant performer. Bernstein spotlighted him on a television show that raised money for Lincoln Center.

Although Ma has graced concert stages worldwide, many younger Americans know him from *Mr. Rodger's Neighborhood* and *Sesame Street*. He has sought to demystify classical music and broaden its appeal.

Others might remember him, however, for the time he left one of his cellos, worth more than two million dollars, in the trunk of a New York City taxicab. (He got it back.)

Ma, with some fifty recordings and more than ten Grammys, is indisputably a classical superstar—and now an American citizen.

* * *

Colin Powell
First African-American secretary of state

Colin Powell, secretary of state, four-star general, and former chairman of the Joint Chiefs of Staff, was born April 5, 1937, the son of Jamaican immigrants Luther and Maud Powell.

He was raised in a poor, integrated neighborhood in the South Bronx. Powell went to public school eventually graduating from the City College of New York. His military career began at CCNY when he joined the Reserve Officers Training Corps there.

To this day he remains a devout supporter of public education.

"I owe an unpayable debt to the New York City public education system," Powell wrote in his 1995 autobiography *My American Journey*. "I typified the students that CCNY was created to serve, the sons and daughters of the inner city, the poor, the immigrant. If the Statute of Liberty opened the gateway to this country, public education opened the door to attainment here. I am, consequently, a champion of public secondary and higher education. I will speak out for them and support them for as long as I have the good sense to remember where I came from."

After his college graduation, he entered the army as a second lieutenant. He was sent twice to Vietnam. He received two Purple Hearts, a Bronze Star, a Soldier's Medal, and the Legion of Merit during his service there. He once escaped a helicopter crash only to return to the burning wreckage to rescue three men, one of who was his commanding general.

His intelligence and hard work took him through the ranks until in 1987, President Ronald Regan appointed him national security adviser.

President George Herbert Walker Bush appointed him chairman of the Joint Chiefs of Staff, the top military adviser to the president, in 1989.

Columnist Carl Rowan wrote of Powell's appointment, "To understand the significance of Powell's elevation to this extremely difficult and demanding post, you must realize that only a generation ago it was an unwritten rule that in the foreign affairs field, blacks could serve only as ambassador to Liberia and minister to the Canary Islands."

Powell later admitted, "I confess that I also felt along with the pride, a certain burden to prove myself as the first African-American to hold the position."

As chairman of the joint chiefs, Powell successfully supervised the planning for the Persian Gulf War.

After the election of George W. Bush in 2000, Powell was appointed secretary of state.

The American dream is something Colin Powell has given much thought.

"Our Constitution and our national conscience demand that every American be accorded dignity and respect, receive the same treatment under the law, and enjoy equal opportunity," he wrote.

He also noted, "We have to start thinking of America as a family. We have to stop screeching at each other, stop hurting each other, and instead start caring for, sacrificing for, and sharing with each other. We have to stop constantly criticizing, which is the way of the malcontent, and instead get back to the can-do attitude that made America. We have to keep trying, and risk failing, in order to solve this country's problems."

He discussed his love for America, saying, "It is a love full of pride for our virtues and with patience for our failings. We are a fractious nation, always searching, always dissatisfied, yet always hopeful. We have an infinite capacity to rejuvenate ourselves. We are self-correcting. And we are capable of caring about each other. We will prevail over our present trials. We will come through because our founders bequeathed us a political system of genius, a system flexible enough for all ages and inspiring noble aspirations for all time."

PART III

If it's not broke, don't try to fix it—but if it is, roll up your sleeves, open the toolbox, and get to work

CHAPTER SIX
Tax-code quagmire

It started simply enough.

Fourteen and 11,400.

Those were the number of pages and words in the tax code of 1913, instituted after ratification of the Sixteenth Amendment, giving Congress the "power to lay and collect taxes on incomes, from whatever source derived."

The provisions were simple, as well.

If you made more than $3,000 a year, you paid 1 percent to Uncle Sam. More than $20,000, a slightly higher rate. And then if you were lucky enough to have an income of more than $500,000, you were bumped to a whopping 7 percent.

Guess what. All this was reported to the government on a four-page form–one page of instructions, one eight-line page summarizing your income and deductions along with the tax computation; a 12-line page detailing your income; and a seven-line page listing deductions.

Compare that to the mess we have today. The U.S. tax code runs an astonishing 11,760 pages with more than thirteen million words. (Albert Einstein, no slouch in the brainpower department, observed that "the hardest thing in the world to understand is the income tax," and he said that years ago in a far less-complicated tax time.)

Taxpayers today are buried in 70 different tax forms. If you're lucky, it only takes you thirteen hours to complete the 1040 form. But more than 90 percent of Americans hire it to a professional to compute their taxes. No wonder Henry Bloch, founder of that ubiquitous tax-preparation chain, said, "Every time the government changes things, business does increase.

Every year a few more people throw up their hands and say 'I can't prepare my own return anymore.' "

It's not only accountants and tax attorneys who benefit from the complicated tax code. Consider this. In 1913 the Internal Revenue Service had 3,000 employees. By the end of the century? Try 115,000. That's about the size of Stamford, Connecticut. That's more than all the employees working for the Drug Enforcement Agency; Environmental Protection Agency; Food and Drug Administration; Occupational Safety and Health Administration; Bureau of Alcohol, Tobacco and Firearms; and the FBI combined.

On top of that, the IRS is viewed with distrust and fear by many Americans. And why not when you consider the testimony in congressional hearings in 1997 and 1998 as example after example of agency abuse was revealed?

How else can what happened to John Colaprete be described than abuse? Mr. Colaprete owned a restaurant in Virginia Beach, Virginia. He testified that when he discovered his bookkeeper had embezzled $40,000, he fired her. The former employee then went to the IRS claiming that Colaprete and his restaurant manager were engaged in gun running, drug dealing, and money laundering. After only a forty-eight hour investigation, teams of armed IRS-Criminal Investigation Division agents showed up simultaneously at the restaurant and the homes of Colaprete and his manager. Colaprete's front door was torn off its hinges, his personal papers seized. They even took his dog.

The manager was ordered out of a shower, and his teenage son was ordered to lie on the floor by gun-wielding agents. The upshot? Charges were never filed against Colaprete and his manager. Four months later, the impounded records were unceremoniously dumped on the sidewalk in front of the restaurant. The bookkeeper was jailed for embezzling other employers.

And Colaprete did not receive so much as an apology from the IRS. Little wonder the word "Gestapo" was heard at the hearings.

But IRS actions can be about much smaller alleged infractions.

One tax attorney recounted the story about a client who owned a small beauty salon. The IRS claimed she owed $175 in unpaid taxes. A lien was put on her business, and its contents put up for auction. Although the woman produced a canceled check showing she had paid the money, the auction went on as scheduled, not only destroying her business, but causing her public humiliation.

The attorney subsequently proved that an IRS computer error had entered the tax due twice. The woman did not owe the additional money. Did that make a difference? No. The IRS hid behind the statute of limitations and refused to repay the excess tax that it had collected by the sale of her property.

Keep in mind that while in most venues in this country, you are considered innocent until proven guilty. With the IRS, there is no such presumption. You have to prove you're innocent. It's little wonder many Americans would like to get rid of the IRS altogether.

* * *

There has been a lot of talk over the years about "reform" and "simplification," but to date, neither has occurred. The tax code has been changed more than thirty times over forty years, and it has only gotten more complicated. The 1997 tax bill added 600 pages to the code. (The joke around Washington was that the big winners in the tax bills weren't big corporations getting breaks and certainly not the average taxpayers, but rather accountants and tax lawyers. So what else is new?) No one less than former IRS Commissioner Shirley Paterson said, our "income tax system is an unwieldy, inefficient, ungodly mess." And who would know better?

Unfortunately, we would, the taxpayers.

One-time presidential candidate Steve Forbes called the tax code "a monstrosity, and there's only one thing to do with it. Scrap it, kill it, drive a stake through its heart, bury it, and hope it never rises again to terrorize the American people."

We have reached a point, as Walter B. Wriston, former CEO of Citicorp, put it, that "all the Congress, all the accountants and tax lawyers, all the judges, and a convention of wizards all cannot tell for sure what the income tax law says."

Maybe it's time we took the advice of Peter Finch's character in the movie, *Network*. "Go to the window, open it and stick your head out, and yell, 'I'm mad as hell, and I'm not going to take this anymore!'"

President Ronald Reagan once quipped, "The taxpayer—that's someone who works for the federal government, but doesn't have to take a civil service examination."

President Reagan may have been joking, but at the same time, he was fingering a fundamental problem with our tax system as it has evolved. You know what? We're not supposed to be "working" for the government. It's supposed to be working for us.

An insidious side effect of this "unwieldy" setup has been the creation of an underground economy. It's impossible to accurately estimate, but the guesstimate is that billions of dollars go unreported because the plumber, electrician, and wholesaler are being paid in cash.

Former network anchor David Brinkley observed, "The American people as taxpayers have begun in wholesale numbers to cheat, out of resentment of a tax system they think is unfair, too complicated, and wasteful of their money. The so-called underground economy is growing rapidly—people working for cash only, reporting nothing, paying nothing."

In 2000, Mississippi Senator Trent Lott addressed the national tax debate. "With the April 15 tax filing deadline just behind us," he wrote, "you're probably perturbed about the entire tax experience. Every year we dread our tax system' complexity—the costs of having our taxes done or the time-consuming effort of doing them ourselves. Many of us question parts of our tax system's rationale, and it is with very good reason. ...The time is obviously right for a national tax debate."

And judging by a *Parade* magazine poll of a few years back, Lott couldn't be more on target. Fifty to one, readers voted to get rid of the present code—and that was the sentiment of hundreds of IRS agents. (It is a sad commentary on our tax system when the IRS telephone assistance program was found to be giving out wrong answers to more than eight million callers. If trained IRS personnel can't figure out the code, how can the average citizen be expected to?)

So the question is "What to do?"

Steve Forbes has it right. Send what we have to the dumpster. Our tax code is outmoded and outdated. Throw away this garbage and start afresh.

President George W. Bush campaigned on a platform of tax change. His administration was able to get passed the Economic Growth and Tax Relief Reconciliation Act of 2001, a compromise that called for $1.35 trillion in tax cuts over eleven years, estate tax repeal, marriage penalty relief, education incentives, child tax credit increase, pension reform, and alternative minimum tax relief.

And as well meaning a victory it was for the American taxpayer, it still was not a solution. Do we really want as a system what Will Rogers said "has made more liars out of the American people than golf has. Even when you make a tax form out on the level, you don't know when it's through if you are a crook or a martyr"?

* * *

Complaints, complaints. Are there any alternatives?

You betcha.

A flat tax.

A national sales tax.

A value added tax.

All three have pros and cons. All three are infinitely better than what we have.

What is this flat tax? Real simple. Everyone pays 15, 16, 17—let the economists pick the right number—percent of income. Bottom line. That's it. No deductions. No loopholes. One flat percentage, for everyone.

As it is, the national average is 22 percent. A flat tax would mean more money for many Americans, more money for them to save, invest, and spend. More money to boost the economy and keep it strong.

One benefit would be throwing away the mountain of forms and dispensing with the megahours of tax preparation. It is estimated that a flat-tax system would reduce paperwork to ten lines on a postcard.

Flat tax would deep-six all those complex corporate depreciations. As it is, companies looking for tax reductions make decisions that hurt their long-term viability and profits. Businesses forgo building a new plant because of negative tax implications. This is wrong. It deprives companies growth. It deprives communities revenues. It deprives workers new jobs.

Under a flat-tax system, income would be taxed once—when you earn it. There would be no more double-dipping by taxing savings, investments, or inheritance.

So what, proponents argue, if a flat tax doesn't completely put the IRS out of business? It would transform it from the 800-pound gorilla on the taxpayer's back to a manageable chimpanzee.

* * *

The second alternative to the current muddle of a code is a national sales tax. Such a tax would mean the end of the income tax—and no more IRS. The national treasury would collect sales tax revenue as state treasuries do.

Forget about how much you earn. A national sales tax depends on how much you spend.

That underground economy, which includes noncitizens living in this country who enjoy all that we have to offer, but pay little for that luxury, not to mention the illegal aliens, would now contribute to the national coffer by a tax on what they buy.

Throw into the mix that we spend some $600 million in trying to comply with our present tax code—money not spent on growing our economy—and a national sales tax shows a lot of merit.

Harvard economist Dale W. Jorgenson estimates that "switching to either a national sales tax or flat tax would add about $2.5 trillion to national wealth."

* * *

This brings us to a third alternative—the value added tax.

The VAT, in effect for years in many countries around the world including the European Economic Community, is a variation on the sales tax. Instead of one tax at the time of purchase, taxes are charged every time an item, in the production chain, becomes more valuable. Say ore is mined and sold to a refiner. Five percent is added to the purchase price. The metal now goes to a manufacturer. Another 5 percent is tacked on, and so on.

While the final cost of the product would be higher than it is now, that seems justified when you consider the elimination of the IRS and its monumental budget. The country's total revenue needs is built into the cost of goods. Furthermore, exports would not be taxed so as not to price American-made products out of the world market, but all imports would be taxed.

It is estimated that the cost of compliance of this tax structure would be about 100 times less than what we have now. According to Trent Lott, "compliance [filing accurate tax returns on time] alone for the current code cost American taxpayers an estimated $225 billion in 1996, or about 15 percent of taxes collected that year."

It doesn't make sense to keep the status quo. It is way past time to heed Lott's call. "Some people support a flat tax. Others say we should eliminate the IRS and start again. Still others say we shouldn't go that far. I'm simply saying let's put taxes on the table and begin this vital national discussion."

And do something–fast.

* * *

Some random thoughts on taxes and the American tax system.

"The nation ought to have a tax system which looks like someone designed it on purpose."

–William E. Simon, former secretary of the treasury

"The United States is the only country where it takes more brains to figure your tax than to earn the money to pay it."

–Edward J. Gurney, Florida senator, 1969-1975

"We have from time-to-time complained about the complexity of our revenue laws and the almost impossible challenge they present to taxpayers or their representatives. . . . Our complaints have obviously fallen upon deaf ears."

–Arnold Raum, senior U.S. Tax Court judge

"It's a game. We [tax lawyers] teach the rich how to play it so they can stay rich–and the IRS keeps changing the rules, so we can keep getting rich teaching them."

–John Grisham, lawyer, author of *The Firm*

"If Thomas Jefferson thought taxation without representation was bad, he should see how it is with representation."

–Rush Limbaugh, radio talk show personality

"When there is an income tax, the just man will pay more and the unjust less on the same amount of income."

–Plato, *The Republic*

"Income tax returns are the most imaginative fiction being written today."

–Herman Wouk, author of *The Caine Mutiny*

"This is the season of the year [April 15] when we discover that we owe most of our success to Uncle Sam."

–*Wall Street Journal*

I believe we should all pay our tax bill with a smile. I tried, but they wanted cash.

–Anonymous

"Collecting more taxes than is absolutely necessary is legalized robbery."

–Calvin Coolidge

"We have allowed taxes and inflation to rob us of our earnings and savings."

–President Ronald W. Reagan, in his second inaugural address, January 1985

CHAPTER SEVEN
Why Johnny and Joanie still can't read

"Children are one quarter of our population and 100 percent of our future."

—First Lady Laura Bush

Let me tell you a story.

It takes place about seventy years ago. A teacher in the New York City public school system had devised a method for getting across the lessons of As and Bs, pluses and minuses, verbs and adjectives to her students.

In the morning, she taught, and the children listened. At noon, a student would bring her a cup of hot water for her bouillon cube. When the students came back from their lunch–some sooner than others–they would find the afternoon's assignment neatly written on the blackboard. They quickly set about getting it done.

Starting at 1:10, a line formed in front of the teacher's desk. She carefully read through each student's answers. If she found so much as one mistake, no matter how small, the student was sent back to his or her desk to redo the entire assignment. If Johnny was smart, he was done at 1:15, and the rest of the afternoon was his, to read, to study, even to go home.

Teacher did not leave until every student produced an error-free assignment, which sometimes meant staying until 4:30 or 5. In this way the children learned reading, writing, and arithmetic. They also learned valuable lessons in perseverance, responsibility, good conduct, and self-control.

Where are such teachers today? What happened to American education, once hailed and held up as an example for all to emulate? Now too many children are receiving inferior schooling. They are being promoted and sent to college without mastering the basics when in that teacher's classroom of seventy years ago they weren't allowed out the door to go home until they mastered their lessons. Major universities have been reduced to giving remedial reading courses to incoming freshmen.

The Organization for Economic Cooperation and Development (OECD) conducted a study in 2000 rating the ability of fifteen-year-olds in various countries to apply what they learned in reading, mathematics, and science.

American students only placed in the middle of the pack. In reading, fourteen nations scored higher than the U.S. (Finland, Canada, New Zealand, Australia, Ireland, Korea, the United Kingdom, Japan, Sweden, Austria, Belgium, Iceland, Norway, France.) We ranked eighteenth in math and fourteenth in science.

U.S. Secretary of Education Rod Paige disparaged our results as mediocre. "In the global economy, these countries are our competitors. Average is not good enough for American kids."

Many reasons have been offered for the falling performance of American students. Some blame television. It's estimated that children ages six to eleven spend twenty-three hours a week in front of the television set. That falls only slightly to twenty hours for twelve- to seventeen-year-olds.

Others point to the trend in the sixties and seventies away from required courses, the basics, to allowing high school students to take many electives. Some say there has been a "dumbing down" of curriculum and standardized exams to get the kids out the door with a diploma.

Is it the fault of parents for not pushing their children more and not insisting on serious study habits? Inferior teachers who are ill prepared to teach? Principals who don't lead? School boards who don't supervise? Overcrowding?

The answer to why Johnny and Joanie can't read is all of the above. Now the question is how to solve the problem.

First lady Laura Bush, a former public school teacher and librarian, has taken on the crusade of improving the state of American education. She is a great proponent of early learning, "crib to classroom," as she puts it. "The first five years of life are a critical time for children to develop the physical, emotional, social, and cognitive skills they will need for the rest of their lives."

"Before President Bush and I married," she has said, "we had a couple of theories on raising kids. Now we have a couple of kids and no theories. But one thing we know for sure: What a child experiences from day one to grade one has a direct and profound impact on his future and on our future."

First and foremost, she and many experts in the field advocate that parents and caregivers read to children. This develops language skills that will carry them prepared into the classroom. As good as television shows such as "Sesame Street" are, it's the voice of the live reader and the interaction—questions, responses, recognizing the need for explanation—that makes that learning experience superior.

As Laura Bush explains, "Some parents and caregivers may not realize how important it is to make time for language and literacy-building activities. They may think that is the job of the preschools and early childhood centers or that television is a good substitute."

Young children should be encouraged to start reading simple books with the help of their parents. It has been shown that a tenth-grader's reading score can be accurately predicted by how well he knows the alphabet on entering kindergarten.

It is also believed that adults should keep on reading to children even after the child has learned to read. Into middle school, books above the child's reading level should be chosen with slightly advanced vocabulary. In this way, the parent can share the experience of a good book while also teaching.

Another factor in effective crib-to-classroom learning is good preschools, which should be available to all kids despite their parents' ability to pay. The accomplishments of Head Start show why.

Started in 1965 under Lyndon Baines Johnson, it received $130 million in federal funds from George W. Bush in his No Child Left Behind Act, passed with an overwhelming majority in 2001

Initially it was an eight-week summer program, the aim of Head Start was to break the stranglehold of poverty through education. By 2001, more than twenty million children benefited from early teaching.

The astonishing statistics of Head Start shows why its backing crosses party lines and supports Laura Bush's belief that early childhood education is paramount.

The program has served more than twenty million "at-risk" children from low-income and poverty-level families. They live in inner-city neighborhoods where it's easier to buy crack cocaine than a cup of coffee, in hardscrabble, failed-crop rural communities, and in untended pockets of suburbia. Head Start makes them "Ready to Read, Ready to Learn," as Mrs. Bush calls her early education initiative.

The program also gives its young students a leg up on life.

- One-third more at-risk children who attended Head Start graduated from high school than those who did not.

- At-risk children who did not have the benefit of Head Start are five times more likely to be arrested repeatedly by age 27 than those who did.

- Young women who attended Head Start are one-third less likely to be unwed mothers and 25 percent less likely to have children as teenagers, saving the government billions of dollars annually in support.

Head Start kids have also been shown less likely to be left back a grade and more motivated throughout their school career.

To strengthen Head Start, George W. Bush set a goal training the 50,000 teachers in the best prereading and language teaching techniques.

* * *

Once children start elementary school, they are often joined by far too many others in the classroom. Reducing class size is another important step in restoring quality education.

A longtime Philadelphia kindergarten teacher recounted a year when she had only twenty-two students plus a literacy intern to help out. "Many [of the students] wrote and illustrated stories on the computers. Most were able to read in the first-grade level in June....Small class size doesn't mean less work for the teacher, but more personalized education."

She emphasized that "if a child leaves kindergarten reading, that child will be successful in school. If children leave kindergarten and first grade not reading, they will have an almost-impossible chance of ever catching up."

Kindergartens should also last all day. For that matter, the amount of time spent in school should be lengthened for everyone. Increase the number of days in a school calendar from 180 to 240. How many kids today need those three months of summer vacation to help out with the crops?

Year-round education wouldn't necessarily be more expensive. Some students could be attending school while others were on vacation. This would translate into the need for fewer buildings with their attendant costs for maintenance, heating, and personnel.

Also, it's been shown that kids forget things over the summer, which means repeating material in the fall that was covered in the spring. What a waste of time.

* * *

Let's not stop there. The teaching profession has become a mockery. Let's hold teachers and administrators responsible for doing their job. In private industry, if you don't measure up, you get the boot.

George W. Bush wants children in grades three through eight to be tested in math and reading–every year.

This doesn't mean teaching how to take tests to the detriment of other learning. Proponents maintain that tests should accurately reflect curricula. No more multiple-choice English questions. Make the kids read difficult passages and write essay answers demonstrating comprehension.

Give schools an incentive for better performance. Pay them. North Carolina has a system that gives more than one thousand dollars for each staff member if the school meets a specified improvement on state tests. It has worked.

Parents shouldn't be kept in the dark about school performance. Under the 2001 education reform law, states have to provide annual "report cards." Parents will now know how their child's school did on statewide exams and how their child's school–and teachers–measures up.

However, no matter how often you grade a mediocre teacher, that teacher is going to stay mediocre. We may never return to the "good old days" when bright men and women were called to the field. They saw teaching as a noble profession that contributed greatly to society. A fact of the twenty-first century and its market economy is that if you want excellence, you have to pay for it.

In many states, teachers' salaries are abysmally low. And the quality of education in those states reflect that. A 1998 survey by *Education Week* magazine found that teachers between the ages of 44 and 50 with a master's degree earned $30,000 less than people with the same degree in other fields.

Some say that merely raising salaries is simplistic. While it needs to go along with other reforms, it has worked. Take Connecticut. It raised salaries by a third, with the average teacher earning more than $50,000 and the top paid taking home $80,000.

Undergraduates are clamoring to get into the University of Connecticut's teaching program–the school turns away three out of four applicants.

The payoff has been tremendous in terms of the quality of education. The state now ranks first in reading achievement.

School districts also need to stand up to the teachers' unions and get rid of the "single-salary" system. Under that, teachers with the same degree level and seniority get paid the same. No. Better teachers should be paid more.

* * *

If our schools are to get better, parents must be involved on every level. There are the things they must do at home, such as reading to their children and supervising homework. At the schools, they must keep in touch with teachers and track how their kids are doing. And they must watchdog school boards, attend meetings, let board members know what is important to the community.

The Lower Merion school district in suburban Philadelphia was faced with having to make budget cuts. Among those suggested by the superintendent was dropping an elementary school foreign language program. Parents stood up, decrying the move, begging it be reinstated. Some argued that in this new global age, American kids needed to learn foreign languages and elementary school was the best place to begin.

What happened? The administration took another look at the budget and was able to find enough money to keep the program going. It's that kind of involvement and commitment that keeps that district ranked as one of the top in the country with about 95 percent of its graduates going to colleges and universities and many of the remainder attending vo-tech institutions. Not to mention that 5 percent of its high school seniors are named National Merit Scholars.

* * *

Our institutions of "higher learning" could do with some shaking up as well. Start with abolishing the notion of open enrollment that institutions like City College of New York instituted. Apply standards for admission. What had the world come to when Harvard was offering a remedial reading course?

Put integrity back into diplomas. It seems that getting the tuition check is more important to some colleges than teaching their students. Colleges shouldn't be day-care centers for undergraduates because they can pay the freight. Put professors back into the classroom. And make them hand out well-earned grades.

Failure to do so is dishonest, which may explain why graduates leave with degrees in accounting, law, and medicine and a skewed view of morality and ethics. The corrupt atmosphere of the universities boils over into our total society and economy.

* * *

On signing the education act of 2001, President George W. Bush reinforced his commitment that no child be left behind. "These reforms express my deep belief in our public schools and their mission to build the mind and character of every child, from every background, in every part of America."

Improving the American education system, teaching Johnny and Joanie to read, won't be easy. But it must be done if we are to stay the great and preeminent nation we are.

* * *

Laura Bush speaking to the Organization for Economic Cooperation and Development (OECD) Forum, May 14, 2002

I thank the many OECD member country ambassadors who are here today. This year's forum focuses on four themes: security, equity, education, and growth. All four are important—and I believe all four hinge on one: education. Education opens the door of hope to all the world's children.

Friends and distinguished guests, no matter what country you call home, no matter what our differences in culture or custom or faith, one value transcends every border: All mothers and fathers the world over love their children and want the very best for them.

As President Bush said earlier this year in his State of the Union address to Congress: "All fathers and mothers, in all societies, want their children to be educated, and live free from poverty and violence . . . , No nation owns these aspirations, and no nation is exempt from them."

. . . Education can help children see beyond a world of hate and hopelessness. With education comes greater self-respect and respect for others. With education comes greater understanding and tolerance.

. . . Our public schools are open to every child in America, and we

are working to make sure they provide a quality education to every child. The United States Congress recently passed, and my husband signed into law, the most sweeping public education reforms in a generation.

The initiative is called "No Child Left Behind" and is based on the principles of accountability and results. The new law sets high standards and holds schools accountable for achieving them. It requires states and school districts to test students and publish the results, so parents know which schools are performing—and which ones are not. The law gives local school districts greater flexibility to achieve results, and it empowers parents and students with more information and more choices.

Providing a quality education for our children begins with putting first things first, and in education, reading always comes first. Reading is the first step to learning. So that all our children can achieve their dreams, my own country, and countries around the world, must do a better job of teaching children to read.

Children who can read have a greater chance of succeeding in school—and in life. According to a recent study from the OECD, at least 15 percent of the world's 15-year-olds can read only at the most basic level, and in some countries, that number is as high as 30 percent.

A parent is a child's first reading teacher. The early years of a child's life are critical to lifelong learning, so President Bush has announced an early childhood initiative called "Good Start, Grow Smart."

This initiative will strengthen and improve our Head Start preschool education programs by including early literacy, language, and number skills. It will help preschools coordinate with elementary schools to make sure children enter school with the prereading and language skills necessary to succeed. And the initiative will provide parents and caregivers with the latest information about early literacy and teaching strategies.

Research shows what parents have always known, and that is:

When parents hold babies in their arms and sing to them or talk to them, they help babies grow both physically and emotionally. This interaction establishes a strong bond between parent and child, and it promotes a child's happiness and self-confidence.

Research also shows that it is very important for parents to read to their children from the time that they are babies. Children who are read to early and often learn two things: First, that reading is important, and second, that they are important.

Before children are old enough to attend school, they should learn basic vocabulary words. Also, they should begin to recognize the letters of the alphabet and understand the sounds that correspond to those letters. If children start school with this knowledge, they are much more likely to succeed in school.

For example, reading scores for tenth-grade students in the United States can be predicted with surprising accuracy based on a child's knowledge of the alphabet in kindergarten. A growing body of scientific research is providing new information about the best and most effective way to teach reading, and we are eager to share that information with parents, teachers, and all who care for children.

Another priority of mine is recruiting quality teachers. One of the most immediate and effective ways to improve education is to achieve President Bush's great goal: a quality teacher in every classroom. The United States will need two million new teachers during the next ten years. I am working with a variety of organizations to encourage recent college graduates, career professionals, and retiring military personnel to bring their skills to America's classrooms.

Teachers deserve our respect and appreciation. Teachers have one of the most important jobs in any society because they help shape and mold our future.

A young girl named Amy, from the state of Texas, wrote this to me: "The reason why my teachers deserve to be appreciated is because they go above and beyond what most people do. They get up early in the morning, make breakfast, get dressed, go to school, teach, go home, eat, grade papers, and make lesson plans, and then go to bed. The next day is more of the same. They spend their own money to get things to make learning fun for kids. They work more time for less pay doing something they love to do. They try to make a difference."

Teachers do make a difference. Most of us can remember a childhood teacher who especially inspired or encouraged us. My favorite was my second-grade teacher. I admired her so much that I decided to become a teacher. The years I spent in the classroom were among the most fulfilling years of my life.

By preparing children to learn to read, recruiting quality teachers, setting high standards, and holding schools accountable for results, we prepare our children to succeed—and open the doors of prosperity and opportunity.

A former President of the United States said that where knowledge spreads, wealth spreads; and to diffuse knowledge in the world is to diffuse wealth in the world. Those words were spoken by President Rutherford B. Hayes on May 15, 1878, and they are as true today as they were 124 years ago.

Those who acquire knowledge have a better opportunity to acquire wealth, and the truly knowledgeable human being also desires to be a better neighbor, citizen, and student of the world. Education is the most important long-term investment we can make in the future, because through education, all the world's children have a far better chance of pursuing their dreams in peace and prosperity.

CHAPTER EIGHT
Bad business

"The business of America is business."

So said Calvin Coolidge in 1925.

Enron. WorldCom. ImClone. To name a few companies that seared across the headlines.

Why does it seem that at the beginning of the twentieth-first century, the business of America is bad business?

Arbitrageur Ivan Boesky was applauded by the graduating class of Berkeley's business school in 1985 when he proclaimed "greed is healthy. You can be greedy and still feel good about yourself."

Later on, the Gordon Gekko character in the movie *Wall Street* shortened that to "Greed is good."

No.

Maybe a little bit of greed is okay, but too much is an indictable offense.

Webster's defines greed as an excessive or rapacious desire for wealth or possessions. This is not a good thing. In fact, the Bible rated it as one of the seven deadly sins.

The word greed doesn't come close to describing the predators on the top of the Enron food chain.

Maybe they forgot that the stockholders own the company. It didn't matter to them as long as they could rake in the money.

Here was a company that basically was nothing more than a middle-man, shuffling energy around the country. If anyone took more than a most cursory pass at the books, maybe its auditors (in this case, read Arthur Andersen) would have noticed that Enron was taking energy out of California, creating a demand, and bringing it back to resell at higher prices. The SEC hadn't bothered examining Enron since 1997. Maybe it was bedazzled by *Fortune* magazine naming Enron the most innovative company in America for six years.

When this house of lies and disinformation showed signs of crumbling, what did these mighty leaders of Enron do?

Twenty-nine insiders dumped $1.1 billion in company shares (with CEO Ken Lay taking a $104 million cut of the pot) and watched as stockholders and employees, who were so naive as to believe these corporate pirates were acting in their best interest, saw life savings and retirement hopes sucked into a greed cesspool.

What is "good" or "healthy" about that?

There was a shell game going at WorldCom. Move $3.9 billion in expenses and make the company look more profitable. This way insiders can sell stock before the company crashes, burns and seventeen thousand workers no longer have a paycheck. But WorldCom CEO Scott Sullivan manages to walk away with $45.4 million after selling company stock before cooked books are discovered.

Americans are losing confidence. In the scandals of the 1980s, Boesky; Charles Keating, of savings-and-loan infamy; Michael Milken, Boesky's buddy on insider trading deals, were rogue individuals. At the beginning of the twenty-first century, we're confronted with rogue megacorporations and good chunks of entire industries.

All for profit.

Not that there is anything wrong with profit. It's the lifeblood of our economy. But profit is good only when it is made fairly and ethically. Bridgestone-Firestone had received reports for years of defective tires, especially on SUVs. The National Highway Transportation Safety Board (NHTSA), the government watchdog, had gotten complaints as far back as 1990. But a recall of 6.5 million Firestone tires wasn't instituted until some ten years later–after sixty-two deaths and 100 injuries.

Workers at one of the manufacturing plants charged that they were ordered to let bad tires go through. One said, "Production took preference over quality . . . it was just always push, push, push."

There are too many headlines about companies selling dangerous products. Ford was in serious financial trouble, which it hoped to pull itself out of with a newly designed SUV, the Ford Bronco II. When it became clear the vehicle had what Ford liked to call a "handling" deficiency, did it stop production and go back to the drawing board? No. It put the Bronco II on the market despite of its rollover problem.

It's not only Ford. From Hyundai to BMW, companies want to cash in on the SUV craze. Sales have skyrocketed. But are they being made safer?

It could be done. Engineers say SUV stability would be improved by lowering the center of gravity and widening the wheel track. But such modifications cost money. So these death mobiles keep rolling off the assembly line and onto American highways.

* * *

Some might argue that driving is inherently a risky business. Should eating be as well?

It is particularly disgusting when the god of greed raises his head in the food business. Some companies would rather save money by not cleaning their processing plants than assuring the health and lives of their customers.

So what is a few dead, here or there?

Is "despicable" a harsh-enough word?

Consider Sara Lee. Many of us grew up with that jingle, "Nobody Doesn't Like Sara Lee," composed by Mitch Lee, who wrote the music for the Broadway musical, *Man of La Mancha*. We thought Sara Lee was this sweet company named after the daughter of the company's founder who liked brownies or something.

Nope. It is a big global company, and one of its smaller divisions was food processing. And one of its plants, which produced Ball Park hot dogs, had to recall products several times in the nineties for unsanitary conditions that allowed for the growth of listeria, a potentially fatal bacterium.

Then in 1998, people started dying in enough numbers to rate the attention of the national press.

According to a *Detroit Free Press* report, managers in "the plant in Western Michigan knew they were shipping tainted hot dogs and deli meats." A federal meat inspector had warned the plant of the danger.

And yet nothing was done–until 21 people died, six women lost their babies, and 101 were sickened.

Because the feds "uncovered no evidence that Sara Lee intentionally distributed the adulterated meat product" the company walked away with a paltry $200,000 fine–less than $10,000 per victim–and had to make a $3-million grant to Michigan State University for food safety research.

Didn't intentionally distribute deadly hot dogs?

The company didn't want to spend the money to keep the facility clean and listeria free. But if the bottom line is going to look better, what are a few lives here or there?

There is a lack of integrity that has overwhelmed America on so many levels, education, big business, how we treat our family and neighbors. In business, take a look at just a very few of the recalls the U.S. Product Safety Commission managed to get in two months in 2002. The CPSC is an independent federal regulatory agency. It acts after getting complaints. With that in mind, think about how long some of these products were on the market before action was taken. Think about how many American consumers paid for items, in good faith, never realizing they were paying for potential death traps.

- Whirlpool Corporation: 1.4 million dehumidifiers because they could overheat, causing a fire hazard.

- Value City and Schottenstein stores, of Columbus, Ohio: 2,300 children's gel candle kits that posed the hazard of melting plastic candleholders included with the kit, causing a fire.

- Eddie Bauer Outlet Stores, of Redmond, Washington: 4,000 stainless steel lunch bottles with a weak seal that could leak hot liquids, posing a serious burn hazard.

- Roto Zip Tool Corporation, of Cross Plains, Wisconsin: 1.9 million handheld saws with handles that could separate from the body, injuring the operator.

- Calphalon Corporation of Toledo, Ohio: 13,000 stainless steel kettles with covers that trap steam inside the kettle causing an increase in pressure, forcing hot water to rise and escape through the spout, posing a serious burn hazard.

- Honeywell Consumer Products of Southborough, Massachusetts: 450,000 moveable baseboard heaters, with heating elements that could short circuit and ignite combustible material under the heater, posing fire and burn hazards.

* * *

Whom can we trust? Our stockbrokers? They give us "knowledgeable" advice on what to buy, often something their firm has some interest in. And they take their commissions and run.

They talk a good game. They've got the research and analysis teams. They can throw "facts" and figures at us, haul out the charts to demonstrate how much we would have earned in the past fifty years if we had invested $100 dollars in such-and-such a stock.

For all the glowing analysis to have come true, you needed to find a truly knowledgeable broker, one who didn't churn out transactions for the sake of his commissions and not your portfolio; he would had to have been working in a firm with utmost moral behavior; and you would have had to purchase the correct stock. For these variables to have converged, you'd have to be living in the Twilight Zone.

It doesn't have to be all that complicated. What you want is a simple, close analysis of where to put your money for tomorrow, where to put your money so you may retire with dignity, where to put your money so that you will have enough to enjoy living the longer lifetime that science and medicine has bestowed you.

Guaranteed instruments might not be glamorous and high-flying, but they don't crash and burn, either.

Here's the soundest financial advice you're going to get, and you're getting it for the price of this book.

Put your money in:

- U.S. Treasury bonds;
- Tax-free municipal bonds;
- Tax-deferred annuities where the principal is regulated and often guaranteed by state insurance departments;
- Local banks, where the Federal Deposit Insurance Corporation insures up to $100,000 of an individual or business' account per bank. Interest rates may be low, but you are receiving a return on your principal, which won't be decimated by a rapacious CEO raiding the company you've invested in.

Remember what humorist Will Rogers once said. "I am concerned about the return of my money, not necessarily the return on my money."

* * *

As long as we're talking about planning for the future, let's talk life insurance.

It's human nature to seek security. Life is filled with the unexpected. The one certainty is death, and only its timing is uncertain.

So along comes the life insurance industry, looking to make big bucks by selling you policies you don't need.

I cover a great deal on this matter of buying life insurance in several of my past books, particularly the one titled *How Your Life Insurance Policies Rob You.*

The general concept that you must remember in your need for life insurance is to buy what is commonly known as term life insurance and not any of those fangled, fancy names that only add premium dollars that become a ripoff of you.

But the insurance companies don't want you to know this. They make money bamboozling the public, writing policies not even they understand, and hoping real reform gets stymied by their lobbyists in the halls of Congress.

For years I've been calling for federal, not state by state, regulation of the insurance industry. One-stop regulation would be cheaper and more effective.

* * *

Unfortunately, malfeasance is not the sole domain of big business. We're being bombarded by it all the time. Have you checked your sales slip lately from the local supermarket? Have you counted your change when leaving all registers? What can we do? The best thing we can do is be more alert and more concerned about our dollars.

And we must be more concerned and diligent about whom we choose as our professionals. We must look for more honest and moral people whom we can trust.

You're to blame if you don't question your accountant and lawyer's "billable hours." Are they really working for you, or are they counting the time they spend "thinking" while showering? There's an old joke about a thirty-six-year-old lawyer finding himself standing before Saint Peter at the Pearly Gates.

"But Saint Peter, I don't understand," the lawyer said. "Why now? I'm so young."

Saint Peter glanced done at some papers and replied, "Oh, based on your billable hours, we thought you were ninety-five."

Demand that you receive what you pay for.

Are you seeing a dentist who is X-ray happy because it pads his bill? What about your doctor? Do you want someone who writes out prescriptions willy-nilly because it's easier than finding out what's wrong with you?

And are we checking what our medical professionals are charging the insurance companies? Were the services actually rendered to you. The Social Security Administration is asking all citizens to be more alert about what they are being charged. In the end, it is you and I and all of us who pay through the nose for dishonesty.

$ saved = $ earned

$ not squandered = $ earned

$ not pilfered = equals $ earned

all this adds up to money for you

There are many good, competent professionals out there. Take care, use common sense, and you should be able to find some that aren't crooks.

CHAPTER NINE

Health-care hell

Patient: the American health-care system

Condition: grave

Prognosis: poor, unless undergoes major surgery

Back in the nineteenth century, the medical profession was looked upon with scorn and disgust.

On hearing his son wanted to be a surgeon, a father in 1832 said, "If I had known this, I certainly would not have sent you to college . . . it is a profession for which I have the utmost contempt. There is no science. There is no honor to be achieved in it; no reputation to be made."

The father's attitude is more understandable when you consider that at least one doctor of the time took to robbing trains as a sideline.

Respectability came slowly. But it did come. By the midsection of the twentieth century, the family doctor was something of an icon. He or she cared for you from cradle to grave. He took your temperature when you were a kid, made sure you got your vaccinations on schedule, kept after you to exercise and keep your weight down, got you to a specialist when needed, was at your bedside at the hospital–checking the charts, making sure the medications were correct–in sickness and in health. He knew your family history, and he kept all your records.

It was one-stop medicine.

Today medicine is all about going to one doctor, being sent across the street to another, then to the next county to a specialist who will always find this, that, and the other thing wrong.

Of course, as seductive as one-stop medicine sounds today, this setup had its limitations. The patient had to be confident in his physician's diagnoses. He had to rely on his physician to keep up-to-date on medical advances. And the patient had to have the wherewithal to pay.

With the arrival of new drugs and advanced procedures, doctoring became more expensive. In 1918 a family living in Ohio had an annual medical bill of about $50. Today a single office visit will cost you that and more.

Enter the era of insurance and HMOs.

In the early days of health insurance (it was originally called "sickness" insurance), people were compensated for lost wages, not for their medical bills. Before the 1920s, there wasn't the demand for such insurance since hospital stays and procedures were at a minimum. Hospitals were where you went to die, not get better. Invasive surgery was an almost-certain death certificate. If you needed treatment, you got it in your home, with a doctor coming to minister you there. The home was even where surgery was performed. The doctor didn't charge much. His fees were easy to pay out of pocket.

That started to change in the 1920s. As people increasingly moved to cities, more women were working outside the home, giving them less time to care for sick relatives. Then, too, there wasn't as much living space in cities. There was no place to put ill Great-Aunt Milly.

Medicine was becoming a science. Doctors had to go through tougher medical schools and licensing procedures. New antiinfection techniques were making hospitals safer. People no longer feared them. As Charles E. Rosenberg wrote in *The Care of Strangers*, "by the 1920s . . . prospective patients were influenced not only by the hope of healing, but by the image of a new kind of medicine–precise, scientific and effective."

As good as all this was for the health of the nation, it began pinching the country's pocketbook. The advances cost money.

To ease the pain of payments, the first prepaid insurance plan started in Dallas in 1929. A group of teachers made a deal with Baylor University Hospital. If the teachers coughed up six dollars each, the hospital would provide up to twenty-one days of hospitalization, if needed, for no additional charge. It was a good deal all around. The teachers could stop worrying about a savings-crushing hospital stay, and the hospital had guaranteed income.

Come the Great Depression, and suddenly the Dallas idea looked good to lots of hospitals. Their endowment funding had dried up because of the hard times. The hospitals, to keep running, needed a steady stream of cash.

Next thing you knew, hospitals were banding together, and insurance plans were eventually consolidated into Blue Cross. Doctors watched with wariness. Would the hospitals become so strong that they would start providing doctor services under their plans, stealing patients from outside doctors? The notion of compulsory health insurance was floating around. The specter of doctors being forced to charge fees according to some guideline was raised.

To defend their autonomy, doctors started their own prepaid insurance plan, Blue Shield. Physicians could still charge what they wanted. If Blue Shield didn't pay it all, the patient made up the difference.

The success of the Blues did not go unnoticed in the private sector. There was money to be made in health insurance, and commercial companies soon entered the fray. From 1940 to 1950, the number of insured Americans went from a little more than 20 million to 142 million.

Commercial companies concentrated on insuring healthy employee groups. It was a win-win situation for employees and employers. The former often didn't have to pay income tax on employers' contributions to insurance plans. It was an untaxed pay raise. Employers didn't have a payroll tax on their contributions.

The system was working fine until medical costs skyrocketed in the seventies, coming close to 14 percent of the gross national product. There were many reasons for that.

Inflation.

Bad management and inefficiencies on the part of hospitals, while at the same time they were looking for more profits.

More expensive technology and medications.

The phenomenal rise in the number of specialists.

Doctor abuses such as seeing patients unnecessarily, prescribing unneeded medicines, sending the patients for unnecessary tests because they owned the equipment, anything to create more and more fees.

Little wonder that we started looking for a way to manage these out-of-control costs, which at times were rising at double the rate of inflation.

Enter Richard Nixon and Health Maintenance Organizations, or better known as HMOs. Nixon envisioned HMOs as bringing efficiency and growth to the national health system.

HMOs would set stringent rules covering when a procedure could be performed and how much would be paid. Primary care physicians would no longer send patients trundling off unnecessarily to high-priced specialists. Hospitals would not be allowed to rake in extra money by keeping patients longer than necessary.

The Health Maintenance Organization Act was signed in 1973. By the end of the decade, there were two hundred HMOs in thirty-seven states.

Today 140 million Americans are covered by HMOs or similar managed-care plans.

Was the HMO system the savior of American health care?

Dream on.

Doctors today are dissatisfied. HMOs are second-guessing them and burying them in paperwork. They have to battle HMOs for procedures that in their educated opinion will help patients. More than half of American physicians surveyed in 2000 felt they could no longer provide quality care.

To make matters worse, according to Robert J. Blendon of Harvard University, "many doctors . . . fear this decline in quality will continue."

Patients fear their medical system. Who can blame them when the Institute of Medicine reports that anywhere from 44,000 to 98,000 deaths occur each year because of medical errors? (And critics of this report have the audacity to say the figures are inflated because some of the patients would have died anyway!) In 2001, there were 42,116 traffic fatalities. You were less likely to die on the highway than from a mistake in a hospital because of the sorry lack of quality there and disregard of safety measures.

What is going on when one out of five Americans can point to a medical error that caused suffering to them or a family member? Ten percent of adults say they got sicker after a visit to a doctor's office or hospital.

And many Americans lack confidence in their doctor. We don't have to worry about the pleasant professional whose desire is to treat the patient with dignity. No, the complaints are about the doctor with the god complex, who doesn't listen to his patient, and sometimes won't turn over the patient's own records. Things have gotten so bad that medical schools are now giving "empathy" classes, courses in bedside manners and how to treat the patient with respect. You'd think that should come naturally.

"A good relationship between doctor and patient," explained Dr. Stephen C. Schoenbaum of the Commonwealth Fund, a private, non-profit organization that supports independent research on health and social issues, "characterized by open and trusting communication is a critical component of high-quality health care. Physicians need to understand patients' concerns and circumstances, and patients must feel they have enough time to ask questions and reach agreement on the best course of care and treatment."

Doctors argue HMOs, eager to cut costs, hamstring the patient-physician relationship by micromanaging. As Steve Fishman put it in a *New York* magazine article titled "Medical Malaise," "Now at every turn, insurance companies generate templates that ride herd on [doctors], as if they were unruly kids."

Doctors also complain that they are forced to spend too much time filling out forms, robbing them of time with patients. Ten years ago, one New York doctor had a single assistant. Now he must employ four people to figure out forms from the sixty-four insurance plans he accepts. Each plan has different rules, different codes, different everything.

The reputation of HMOs hasn't been helped by the horror stories of death and misery caused by penny-pinching. Some of these stories make you cringe, others fill you with rage. HMOs argue these are the exceptions, not the norm, that most subscribers are happy with the care they receive.

That is belied by a Commonwealth Fund study that found dissatisfaction with the health care system highest in the United States of all the countries surveyed.

And who's to criticize Americans' malcontent when they read about the eighty-eight-year-old California woman with kidney failure? Her HMO doctor thought she needed dialysis. But wait, that would cost the HMO $40,000 a year. If he prescribed it, it would mean less money for him. So he didn't, and his patient soon died.

Then there was the forty-six-year-old Detroit woman who collapsed getting out of a car. Her husband rushed her to a hospital. Although all efforts were made to save her, she died from a heart attack thirty minutes later.

Imagine how her husband felt a few months later when the HMO refused to pay for the emergency room visit because he hadn't gotten prior authorization. As if you can plan a heart attack. Then there was the infamous "castration" case. The HMO of a seventy-six-year-old ordered him under t⌐ ⌐fe because it was cheaper than getting injections of a drug to keep ⌐state cancer in check.

⌐le a mother is on the phone trying to persuade her HMO to pay for an ambulance, her nineteen-month old suffers seizures.

A thirty-eight-year-old woman dies after her health plan refuses to pay for a promising, government-approved cancer treatment.

An HMO pediatrician suspects a baby girl has cystic fibrosis. He asks the HMO to pay for a $50 test. CF when discovered early is treatable. The HMO would not authorize the test. Shortly after, the baby was admitted to the hospital with pneumonia and collapsed lungs. She died a month later.

The exception, not the rule? Who cares? Doctors should not be given monetary incentives to refuse to do what should be done. HMO employees without medical degrees, who never see the patient, should not be allowed to overrule doctors.

How can this statement (quoted in the *Des Moines Business Record*) by an HMO executive be justified? "We see people as numbers, not patients. It's easier to make a decision. Just like Ford, we're a mass-produced medical assembly line, and there is no room for human equation in our bottom line. Profits are king."

There have been positive effects from HMOs.

As Dr. Bill Barber of Piedmont Hospital in Atlanta put it, HMOs have "forced really a revolution in the way that we take care of our patients. What we've learned is how to manage pain better, we've learned to operate more efficiently, and we've learned how to manage these patients in a way that we can get them home quickly–provided, of course, they're in a safe atmosphere."

Ten years ago, some surgeries meant a five-day hospital stay. Today, the patient can be in the operating room in the morning and safely home by afternoon, saving thousands of dollars.

And by nixing unnecessary operations, HMOs undoubtedly have saved lives.

But the practices of HMOs, the increased overhead from paperwork, and slow reimbursements are not the only reasons some of our best and brightest doctors are leaving the profession to start bed-and-breakfast inns.

They are being crushed financially by exploding malpractice insurance rates. Doctors who have never been sued or have never lost a case are facing onerous increases–if they can get insurance at all. In Pennsylvania, one insurance company after another has pulled out.

In October 2001, 18 orthopedic surgeons in suburban Philadelphia threatened to stop performing surgery. Their malpractice premiums had skyrocketed over two years from $65,000 to $130,000 per doctor.

A Pittsburgh area group of five ob-gyn specialists and a gynecologist who didn't deliver babies saw its premiums go from $78,000 to $286,000 in six years.

Doctors in states like Pennsylvania and Nevada are taking their shingles down, creating severe shortages of doctors in emergency rooms and delivery rooms.

Of course, there's finger-pointing. Doctors blame excessive jury awards and call for tort reform with caps on how much someone can receive for pain and suffering. They also cite venue shopping, where lawyers file a case in, say, Philadelphia where juries are notorious for tremendous awards rather than in the town where the alleged malpractice took place.

Of course the lawyers have a different take on the problem. The fault, they say, lies with insurance companies jacking up prices to make up for losses in the stock market after underpricing policies for years. It's the fault of the doctors, they say, who shouldn't sew up patients with surgical sponges inside them.

* * *

Can anything be done to save our patient, the American health-care system?

Sure.

Let's start with a report card. Let's post, in one, easy-to-find site on the Internet, a report card grading the performance of doctors, hospitals, and HMOs. Don't we have the right to know how many times complaints against an HMO have found to be valid? Shouldn't we know how many times our doctor has been sued for malpractice–and lost? Shouldn't we know the death rate in our hospitals and how many errors for which it has been held accountable?

Obviously rating standards need to be set and explained. For instance, some hospitals have a higher incidence of patients dying after heart surgery because they take riskier cases. But there has to be some quantitative measure of information that will inform the public. We have the right to know. We are, after all, talking about life and death. Ours.

In November 2002, New York State started posting a scorecard rating hospitals with high death rates. Texas, California, Pennsylvania, and New Jersey are also giving the public reports on hospitals. But more needs to be done.

How about this? Electronic prescriptions. Instead of writing out scripts in their notoriously illegible handwriting, doctors check off from a software program the necessary drug and dosage. It gets sent electronically to the pharmacy, and the chance of you, the patient, getting the wrong medication or the incorrect dosage is lessened considerably.

It also means less wasted time (which we all know means less wasted money) calling up doctors to verify what the pharmacist thinks is written. It also saves time for doctors, who sometimes have more than one employee assigned to fielding pharmacy questions.

As long as we're going to have electronic prescriptions, let's have electronic record-keeping. We're in the twenty-first century. Keeping medical records on paper is silly. First of all, without that Doctor Welby keeping all your tests, examinations, inoculations, etc., one doctor doesn't know what the other one is doing or has done.

In 1993 Dr. H. Bleich called paper medical records "an abomination... it is a disgrace to the profession that created it. More often than not the chart is thick, tattered, disorganized, and illegible; progress notes, consultant's notes, radiology reports, and nurses notes are all commingled in accession sequence. The charts confuse rather than enlighten; they provide a forbidding challenge to anyone who tries to understand what is happening to the patient."

In Canada, on birth, you get a health insurance card. For the rest of your life, every time you see a doctor, get medication, are in the hospital, all your health-care activity is recorded in a central data bank. You can move, change jobs, change doctors. Every physician and health-care provider will have your complete medical history.

Step on a rusty nail. When's the last time you had a tetanus shot? It's there for the clinic physician to find. Allergic to codeine? It's there. A family history of strokes? The emergency room staff knows that immediately.

Until an electronic system is instituted, follow the advice of Doctor Marie Savard, who created the Savard System for managing all your health information (*drsavard@comcast.net*). Write down your family history. Childhood diseases. Get every test result. Keep films of MRIs, mammograms, EKGs. You paid for them. They are yours. Keep a list of questions and concerns for your doctor, so that when you go in for an examination, you know what to ask and what is important.

Doctor Savard developed an easy-to-keep binder where you can store all this information.

What else can be done to improve the mish-mash of the American health system?

Say no to HMOs and their medical "assembly lines." Demand that doctors be allowed more time with patients. After all, we're paying the freight. Doctors rightfully contend the more time they can spend with a patient, the better care they can give.

Dr. Savard stopped practicing medicine when she was told she could only have fifteen minutes with each patient. Fifteen minutes? Many patients come in disorganized, discombobulated, and cannot articulate, much less explain, their medical concerns.

Of course, in bean counting, what is overlooked is that when doctors have more time with patients, they can find conditions in early, cheaply treatable stages, saving tons of money. More emphasis should be placed on preventative medicine. For instance, at a time when there should be more education and support for people with diabetes, some hospitals and insurers are cutting back on such programs.

"The money is not there for preventive nutrition and exercise counseling," says Nadine Uplinger, director of the Gutman Diabetes Center at Albert Einstein Medical Center in Philadelphia. "We know if people weighed less and increased their physical activity, the incidence of diabetes could be decreased." And in the long run, money saved.

Here's another idea. The insurance companies might balk, but the country will benefit.

Let's eliminate some of the paperwork. Create a standardized basic policy. Aetna, Cigna, Blue Cross-Blue Shield, all insurance companies would have the same basic coverage. When a patient visits a doctor or enters a hospital, the billing office doesn't have to make calls to figure out what will be paid and what won't. All codes would be the same

Then, if someone wants to pay more, bells and whistles can be added to the policy. But a standardized basic policy–same forms for everyone–would cut down on time and money.

Another benefit for standardization could be coverage for those not below the poverty line, and therefore eligible for Medicaid, but still unable to afford insurance.

Say you lose your job. When you were working, your company and you shared the cost of coverage. Now there is no company, and you're trying to put food on the table. With a nationwide, basic policy, the federal government could pick up the tab for, say, six months or a year, giving you time to find employment. The Germans have been doing something similar for decades, and it works.

Another idea comes from the National Academy of Sciences. Reward good doctors, hospitals, and nursing homes.

In October 2002, the academy recommended that Medicare and Medicaid health-care providers get bonuses based on how good a job they do.

The academy said set standards, judge performance, and pay the good guys 5 to 25 percent more.

Washington can use its clout to upgrade public and private health.

"The federal government should take full advantage of its influential position to set quality standards for the entire health-care sector," Dr. Gilbert S. Omenn of the University of Michigan said.

What else is needed? Passage of a Patients' Bill of Rights. In his 2002 State of the Union address, President Bush reminded Americans that "economic security can vanish in an instant without health security. I ask Congress to join me this year to enact a patients' bill of rights."

Such a bill has been wandering the halls of Congress for years. Among the provisions proponents are seeking would be a guarantee that doctors, not health-plan bureaucrats, would make important medical decisions. The art and science of medicine should return to the people trained in the field.

There would be an independent and binding outside appeals process, in which a patient can make the case he or she was improperly denied benefits.

California's has something along that line already in place. In 2000, the state legislature set up the Department of Managed Health Care. Its job is to handle HMO complaints. When a health plan won't pay for care or doesn't make a decision for more than a month about paying, it will receive a complaint from the department, asking for justification. If a doctor says a procedure is necessary, but the HMO disagrees, the case goes to an independent panel of specialists. Its decision is final.

The bill would also deal with emergency room coverage. Using a "prudent layperson standard," that Detroit man whose wife suffered the heart attack would not have received a bill for ER services because he hadn't gotten the okay from his insurance company first.

While all these suggestions would help, what is needed most is a return of confidence.

Nobody is asking that profits be taken out of health care. All we want is for care to be the priority. We shouldn't be the country that spends the most on health care in the world and be the most dissatisfied with what we receive.

CHAPTER TEN

Whither went justice?

"Make crime pay. Become a lawyer."

–Will Rogers

Q: How many lawyers does it take to change a light bulb? A: Three. One to change it and two to keep interrupting by standing up and shouting "Objection!"

Lawyers do not enjoy a very good reputation in modern-day America. They are perceived by many as going-for-jugular sharks who will do anything to win their case. No matter if their client is guilty, innocent, or has a case with merit.

Lawyers make big bucks, wear thousand-dollar suits, and arrive in chauffeured-driven limousines. This is a misperception. Most lawyers in the United States work in the bowels of the federal bureaucracy or for small and mid-size firms. There is no Johnny Cochran showboating about those who write wills, supervise home sales, or handle property disputes. But because our legal system is so in need of change, its corrupters and manipulators get the spotlight to the detriment of the others.

There are two sides to our legal system–criminal and civil. Both need a good shaking up. The courts are completely clogged. Criminals are not being prosecuted in a timely fashion because there aren't enough judges. Those accused of a crime often know their way around the system. (After all, between 45 and 60 percent of those released from prison return.) These accused ask for trials because they know that as time passes, the state's witnesses might not show up. The accused are rolling the dice that they might luck out and get a lenient judge who will offer them a sweet deal just to get the case off the docket. Or maybe charges will be dropped.

Defense attorneys are more than happy to applaud leniency–because it puts more money in their pockets. Think about it. Getting a client out on the streets more quickly through a plea bargain or reduced sentence, only means he or she may be committing another crime that much sooner–and will need a defense lawyer that much sooner.

There are lawyers who use off-the-wall defenses, with abusive discovery tactics, and file appeals for appeals' sake, not for the purpose of mounting the best defense, but rather for putting more dollars in his bank account.

Meanwhile, taxpayers' dollars are being squandered.

For every 100 convictions, there are sixteen appeals. More court time, more court costs.

The U.S. Constitution lays out the foundation for criminal procedure in the Bill of Rights. We are guaranteed a presumption of innocence, that a defendant must be proven guilty beyond a reasonable doubt, that we may not be made to testify against ourselves, that we are entitled to a speedy trial.

But these procedures should not be distorted and perverted. For one thing, we should make it the law of the land that appeals will be allowed only on the direct guilt or innocence of the defendant. Great rid of these nonsensical procedural gambits. So what if a T wasn't crossed or an I dotted?

While we need more judges to handle the caseloads, we also need an overhaul on how judges reach the bench.

In Colonial days, the king appointed judges, in effect giving him complete control over the judiciary. The Founding Fathers, too, believed in appointed justices, but appointments based on merit. Alexander Hamilton argued against elected judges, saying, "there would be too great a disposition to consult popularity...."

Gradually, more and more states opted for selecting judges in the polling place so that today it's an even split between states with appointments and elections. The latter, however, may lead to abuse. Many people are disturbed by the ramifications of money in campaigns. If you're running for a judgeship, you'll need money to get your candidacy across. And often that money comes from lawyers and firms that will be presenting cases before you.

The question "How would you like it if your opponent in a lawsuit were represented by someone who gave $500 to help the judge get elected" was asked in a report from the American Judicature Society.

Former Texas Supreme Court Justice Bob Gammage points out "people don't pour money into campaigns because they want fair and impartial treatment. They pump money into campaigns because they want things to go their way."

It is not good for the country that people believe elected judges are influenced by their contributors. In Pennsylvania, where all judges are elected, 89 percent of people surveyed held that view.

Supreme Court Justice Anthony Kennedy said in 1999, "This is serious because the law commands allegiance only if it commands respect. And it commands respect only if the public thinks the judges are neutral. And when you have figures like that, the justice system is in real trouble."

On top of which, voters often go into the booth not knowing the names of the candidates, much less their qualifications. It's an eeny-meeny-miney-mo process, just pull the lever for whomever.

So why not bow to the wisdom of the Founding Fathers, why not have universal appointment of justices for long terms from the lowest of courts to the highest?

Let's turn to nominating commissions that make recommendations based on merit. That's what they do in Massachusetts and New Hampshire, where judges serve until age 70. In New York, high-court judges receive 14-year terms, and in Rhode Island, they serve for life.

Federal judges are appointed, and by and large, they outperform those elected in state courts. Let the credentials of local judges be closely scrutinized. Let there be public hearings on their credentials. And then, before they are appointed, let there be a vote by state legislatures, county commissioners, or the borough council who have listened to the testimony.

But that won't completely solve our problems. When those judges are seated, they must take control of their courtrooms. In 1986, the American Bar Association called on judges to "take a more active role in the conduct of litigation; they should see that cases advance promptly and without abuse."

To do that, they are going to need the help of the American taxpayer.

Judges need to have enough money for an adequate number of law clerks and support staff. How can we expect judges to give well-conceived and thoughtful decisions if they don't have the wherewithal to research them?

And how do we expect to attract quality prosecutors when their counterparts on the other side of the aisle, the defense attorney, makes double, triple, or more than they do? Sometimes on the other side of the aisle are public defenders. They, too, must receive enough compensation to draw bright and competent attorneys. There should be justice for all, rich and poor alike.

The idea of higher taxes is an anathema to many, but if they go for a better legal system, then it's time we coughed up.

But that's not the only way the American public must work to improve the system.

Jury duty. Serve when called. Don't search for a way to get out of it.

Thomas Jefferson said, "I consider trial by jury as the only anchor yet imagined by man by which a government can be held to the principles of its constitution."

So what happens when you try to empanel a jury and no one comes? How can we uphold the principles of the constitution?

The excuses that are used to get out of jury duty range from ludicrous to unconscionable. A man falsely tells a judge in a methamphetamine trial that he's a recovering meth addict and believes drug addiction is a disease, not a crime. Another man announces that the defendant looks guilty. Or there's always the "I'm a convicted felon" claim.

We cannot rely on others to be the watchdogs of the system. Sure, it can be boring and tiresome as you sit all day waiting to be picked, only to be sent home. But it is a small price for the well-being of our society.

Of course, people might have more respect for the legal system if it would enforce laws already on the books.

Case in point, the death penalty. It was reinstated in New York in 1995. Since then thousands of thousands of murders have been committed. But has one person been offered the proposition that this law was meant for him or her? Nary a one. No one has been executed.

* * *

Tort: A wrongful act resulting in injury to another's person, property, or reputation, for which the injured party is entitled to seek compensation.

Random House *Webster's College Dictionary*

Seems like a pretty simple proposition. You sell me a car with defective brakes. I get into an accident. You pay. But today, in litigious America with thirty lawyers for every ten thousand people, it has become our "inalienable" right to sue. Too many of us are ready to play the legal lottery and go for that big win.

How else would you explain a family suing the Weather Channel? Why? It missed predicting a storm that roared in during a fishing outing, causing the death of a family member. Or how about the woman who sued Universal Studios because its Halloween Horror Night caused her emotional distress?

Let us not forget the milk shake case. A guy gets into an accident while driving and drinking a milk shake. So what does he do? Sue the fast-food company. Why? Well the company that sold him the drink should have put a label on the container warning against eating and driving.

The guy didn't win, but the fast-food restaurant was out $10,000 in legal fees. The judge refused to make the guy stand that cost because his attorney was "creative, imaginative and he shouldn't be penalized for that."

Some of these cases are beyond ludicrous. A drunk driver, who crashes through detour signs, sues the engineering company that designed the road, the contractor, four subcontractors, and the state highway department. The case goes on for five years, until finally the defendants decide it's the path of least resistance to settle for $35,000. However, the engineering firm's legal fees were $200,000.

No wonder that as governor of Texas, George W. Bush made tort reform a priority and why in the 2000 campaign he included tort reform in his platform. He called for:

- stiffer penalties for "frivolous" lawsuits and imposing a "Three Strikes, You're Out" rule against lawyers who continuously bring these suits;

- amending federal discovery laws to limit "fishing expeditions" and raising the standard for admitting "junk science";

- a "fair settlement rule" stipulating that anyone who rejects a pretrial settlement, then loses the case, would have to bear all costs for both parties, including legal fees.

If you don't think you personally pay for these untoward suits, think again. According to the U.S. Chamber of Commerce, each and every American pays $1,200 a year in "litigation taxes." That's what businesses pass on to you to cover lawsuit costs. That includes millions upon millions of dollars wasted on extra tests ordered by doctors practicing defensive medicine, tests they feel they need to produce in the courtroom if they are sued.

Nobody is suggesting that injured parties not have their day in court. But should a high school basketball star get $100,000 for not being allowed to play following two alcohol-related offenses, including driving under the influence? He and his lawyer seemed to think they had a case under the Americans with Disabilities Act. You see the lad "has been diagnosed as an alcoholic, and that is a recognized disability under federal law," the lawyer said.

There has to be common sense introduced into tort law, with fair caps on rewards. As George Will wrote in 2002, "A right to appropriate compensation for a faulty or harmful product is integral to a property right. But nowadays punitive damages are, as Justice Sandra Day O'Connor says . . . 'limited only by the ability of lawyers to string zeros together in drafting a complaint.'"

It's time we expunged the turpitude from our courts.

It is also time that we insisted that basic law be taught in our schools and universities. As I wrote twenty years ago in *Milton on America*, "The law is for and by its citizens, and we must help to make it work better." And how can we do that if we don't understand it?

* * *

United States Oath of Judicial Office taken by all federal judges

> *"I do solemnly swear that I will administer justice without respect to persons, and do equal right to the poor and to the rich; and that I will faithfully and impartially discharge all duties incumbent on me as according to the best of my abilities and understanding, agreeably to the Constitution and the laws of the United States."*

CHAPTER ELEVEN

Civility starts at home

"A full life is one that serves others, other than yourself"

–George W. Bush,
July 10, 2002

After September 11, for a brief flicker in time, it looked as if the nation's people suddenly remembered how to be civil to one another. The unbelievable heroism of those firefighters and police who rushed up the stairs of the World Trade Center to what they must have realized was certain death had us rushing to give blood and donations to the survivors and the widows and children of the fallen.

But in no time at all, this new civility faded away along with decency and respect for each other.

The nation's been suffering from a tear in our moral fiber for quite some time. It looked as if it had been repaired following that horrific day, but it soon reappeared.

What kind of country is this when obscene gestures are frequent forms of communication? When 75 percent of high school students polled admitted they took part in "serious" cheating? When the president of the United States twists the language, testifying he did not have "sexual relations" with an intern because there was no sexual intercourse involved?

Almost three-quarters of Americans believe that manners are worse today than they were thirty years ago. Travel mass transportation and see how many times a younger person relinquishes his or her seat to a pregnant woman or an elderly person. We are in a land of milk and honey where we grab as much as we can.

How can we improve relations with those beyond our borders when we are in such a state of incivil unrest at home?

Civility does begin at home. Good manners are more than "please" and "thank you." They set the tone for treating others with fairness, consideration, and care. Good manners are the foundation for morality, tolerance, ethics, and character.

Character. Now there's a good, old-fashioned concept. We used to be a nation that took pride in character. Now too many think nothing of tossing it aside if it means a bigger bank balance.

If we're going to turn the tide on our burgeoning incivility, it has to start in the home. Baby Boomer parents have got to learn how to say "no." They must realize their job is to be a parent, not a friend.

It's incredible to realize that 80 percent of people asked by *Time*/CNN thought children were more spoiled in 2001 than they were fifteen or twenty years earlier.

But where's the surprise in that when the Keeping-up-with-the-Joneses has trickled down to child rearing? If the kid down the block has four video game systems and a big-screen TV, by golly, you're not going to deprive little Tommy by giving him any fewer.

Some parents apparently haven't heard the word "overindulgence." How else can you explain a father spending $17,500 to rent New York toy store FAO Schwartz for a night so his 13-year-old daughter and friends could have a slumber party there? What was this guy thinking?

In Houston, some dopey parents spent $20,000 on a catered party for fifty seven-year-olds wearing mink coats like mommy. This is the generation of kids who are quick to point out they're wearing Calvin Klein—when they're still in nursery school.

Obviously, not every parent is doing this, but often even those who can ill afford to do so will cave into a kid's whining for $150 Air Jordan sneakers. It borders on obscene.

But it's the message that gets sent that is most disturbing. The three-year-old screaming for a candy bar in the supermarket. The mother ignoring the child and then giving in. You want it. Whine enough, you get it.

When you get older, you don't have to work for it. Too many kids today aren't expected to do even the smallest chore to help out around the house.

Carrie Fisher, daughter of Hollywood star Debbie Reynolds, admits to one lavish birthday party for her daughter, Billie. "She got an elephant. That's all I have to say. It will never happen again." But Fisher said she saw the light when she overheard Billie brag that her swimming pool was bigger than her friend's. Fisher then set some rules, including having her child clean up her room, something the *Star Wars* star had not done as a youngster growing up in Tinseltown. "I always thought the fairies did it. When I moved into my first apartment, I didn't understand how there were rings in the tub and hair in the sink."

Kids learn by osmosis. They watch. They listen. If they hear you bragging about cheating at tax time, is it so surprising they cheat at test time? A seventeen-year-old from Virginia told CNN, "What's important is getting ahead. The better grades you have, the better school you get into, the better you're going to do in life. And if you learn to cut corners to do that, you're going to be saving yourself time and energy. . . . The better you do, that's what shows. It's not how moral you were in getting there."

With that attitude, there's nothing wrong with paying $10 a page to get a term paper downloaded from the Internet, not if it helps you get a good grade.

But there is something wrong. It leads to the immoralities of the Enrons and ImClones.

Parents should remember they are being watched and their behavior emulated on the sidelines of sporting events. Sports are a great teacher—practice hard, play hard, and you have a chance to succeed. Team sports should build character and teach the value of perseverance. But what is it teaching when parents are going berserk on the sidelines, yelling insults at the refs, getting into fistfights with parents from the opposing team? There was that terrible incident in Massachusetts where two ice hockey fathers got into a fatal fight over whether a foul had been committed—in practice.

The National Alliance of Youth Sports, with 2,200 chapters, reported that there were incidences of parents and coaches involved in abuse, both physical and verbal, at 15 percent of kids' games.

Linda Wacyk, publications editor for Partnership for Learning, wrote, "I'm no psychologist, but I suspect that Field Fury, along with Road Rage, will be hard to eradicate in our stressed-out, uncivil society. But maybe if we each vow to live each day with a little more patience, respect, and self-control, we can start to change our neighborhoods."

Adults need to set a good example, and they need to start teaching their children the difference between right and wrong. Never assume your kids know. Explain your values, that doing the right thing is not a matter of convenience. You get too much change. Don't gloat about it being your lucky day, that if the cashier is that stupid, it's her problem. Give the money back. If you don't, it's stealing, and your kid will know it.

Read to your kids, even after they've learned to read. Pick a book that is a little harder with more complex concepts than they would read on their own. Discuss it with them. Point out behavior you disagree with, explain why it's wrong. And very importantly, listen, really listen to their response. What's black and white to you might be terribly gray to them.

Show your child that helping others is a good thing. If you can volunteer, do so. Remember, lavishing money and gifts on your children is far less important than spending time with them.

In the long run, it won't be the material things you've given your kid that will make him or her happy with a more fulfilling life, it will be the love and wisdom that you've bestowed.

* * *

Aggressive driving and road rage. If you have experienced neither, you haven't been on American roads in the last decade.

- A Jeep Grand Cherokee cuts off a Pontiac Grand Am. The Pontiac driver races after the Cherokee, careening through a residential neighborhood at high speed, before losing control of the car and crashing into an oak tree. Two people die.

- A twenty-two-year-old woman speeds up the right shoulder of a Nevada highway to pass two trucks. She then cuts back onto the road and hits her brakes. To avoid a rear-end collision, one of the truck drivers hits his brake. A motorcyclist smashes into him and is killed.

- At the tollbooths of the Pennsylvania Turnpike, a man feels two women in a compact car have cut him off. Once on the highway, he tailgates them, honking, screaming at them to get over to the right-hand lane so he can pass. The women accelerate to more than 80 miles an hour, trying to get to where they can move over. When they finally can, the road rager deliberately makes contact with their rear bumper, pushing the car off the road. The driver of the compact car dies.

It's a scary proposition pulling your car out of the driveway these days.

The National Highway Traffic Safety Administration (NHTSA) estimates that aggressive driving accounts for 66 percent of traffic fatalities every year.

You know what constitutes aggressive driving. Running red lights. Passing on the right. Tailgating at any and every speed. Cutting back and forth between lanes–often without signaling the lane change. Honking. Speeding up, braking, speeding up, braking. Making threatening hand and facial gestures

According to the NHTSA, aggressive driving results in more than twelve thousand injuries a year. This is a 51 percent increase in aggressive driving incidents since 1990. And to make the situation more worrisome, firearms were used in 37 percent of these incidents, other weapons in 28 percent, and the vehicle was used as a "weapon" in another 35 percent.

The experts will give you all kinds of reasons for the explosion of aggressive driving–the primary cause of road rage, which is a criminal offense. There are more cars on the road. People are more stressed and in a bigger hurry. But some maintain it's a combination of people flat out not knowing how to drive–being ignorant of the rules of the road–and bad manners.

"When we get behind a car, some demon takes over, and we become discourteous, illegal drivers that cause a lot of problems," is how Terry Gainer, director of the Illinois State Police, explains it.

The NHTSA is more specific about who these aggressive drivers are.

- "They are high-risk drivers, more likely to drive impaired, to speed, and/or to drive unbuckled;

- "They are drivers who see their vehicles as providing a cover of anonymity and therefore tend to be less inhibited and more likely to engage in aggressive behavior;

- "They are frequently 'Type A' personalities characterized by high levels of competitiveness, time urgency, irritation, and hostility."

There is one simple step that can be taken to curb aggressive driving. Teach people how to drive. In the 1970s, almost anyone who went for a driver's license had taken a driver's education course. Driver's ed was given in high schools. That's all changed.

"Today our estimate is that that's about 35 percent of the people," said Allen Robinson of the American and Driver Traffic Safety Association. "If people are not aware of what they should do, how do we blame them for what they don't do properly?"

You know what? Hold them responsible. States must pass aggressive driving laws. You break them, you go to driving class or lose your license.

It's pathetic how many people don't know something so basic as who has the right of way at a four-way stop. It's the driver who comes to a complete stop first. But you get those yahoos who think whomever slides through the intersection first without stopping is the one who gets to go. These are the same yahoos who believe a yellow light means hit the accelerator.

The real solution is to go after the root-cause of the problem. And that is civility and respecting your fellow man. Just as we must set an example for our children, set an example for the jerks who drive aggressively. Make a "sorry" sign. Road ragers say they would drop the vendetta if the other driver apologized. It's defensive driving to have a sign that says "sorry" and hold it up to diffuse the situation.

* * *

The bottom line is we must stamp out road rage, family rage, neighbor rage, and citizen rage because that leads to the world rage we're wracked with now. How can we expect to have a civil world if we don't practice civility here?

* * *

Some of George Washington's rules of civility

Every action done in company ought to be with some sign of respect to those that are present.

Show nothing to your friend that may affright him.

Sleep not when others speak; sit not when others stand; speak not when you should hold your peace; walk not on when others stop.

Shake not the head, feet, or legs; roll not the eyes; lift not one eyebrow higher than the other; wry not the mouth, and bedew no man's face with your spittle by [approaching too near] him [when] you speak.

Turn not your back to others, especially in speaking; jog not the table or desk on which another reads or writes; lean not upon anyone.

Be no flatterer, neither play with any that delight not to be played withal.

Read no letter, books, or papers in company, but when there is a necessity for the doing of it, you must ask leave; come not near the books or writings of another so as to read them unless desired, or give your opinion of them unasked-also look not nigh when another is writing a letter.

Let your countenance be pleasant but in serious matters somewhat grave.

The gestures of the body must be suited to the discourse you are upon.

Reproach none for the infirmities of nature, nor delight to put them that have in mind of thereof.

Show not yourself glad at the misfortune of another though he were your enemy.

When you see a crime punished, you may be inwardly pleased; but show pity to the suffering offender.

Superfluous compliments and all affectation of ceremonies are to be avoided, yet where due they are not to be neglected.

Play not the peacock, looking every where about you, to see if you be well decked, if your shoes fit well, if your stockings sit neatly and clothes handsomely.

Associate yourself with men of good quality if you esteem your own reputation; for 'tis better to be alone than in bad company.

Let your conversation be without malice or envy, for 'tis a sign of a tractable and commendable nature, and in all causes of passion permit reason to govern.

Speak not injurious words neither in jest nor earnest; scoff at none although they give occasion.

Be not forward but friendly and courteous, the first to salute, hear, and answer; and be not pensive when it's a time to converse.

Detract not from others, neither be excessive in commanding.

If two contend together take not the part of either unconstrained, and be not obstinate in your own opinion; in things indifferent be of the major side.

Reprehend not the imperfections of others, for that belongs to parents, masters, and superiors.

Think before you speak; pronounce not imperfectly, nor bring out your words too hastily, but orderly and distinctly.

When another speaks, be attentive yourself; and disturb not the audience. If any hesitate in his words, help him not nor prompt him without desired; interrupt him not, nor answer him till his speech has ended.

Be not apt to relate news if you know not the truth thereof.

Undertake not what you cannot perform but be careful to keep your promise.

In disputes, be not so desirous to overcome as not to give liberty to *one to deliver his opinion and submit to the judgment of the major part, specially if they are judges of the dispute.*

Let your recreations be manful not sinful.

Labor to keep alive in your breast that little spark of celestial fire called conscience.

CHAPTER TWELVE
Finding financial freedom

Franklin Delano Roosevelt spoke eloquently of the Four Freedoms:

• freedom of speech and expression;

• freedom of every person to worship God in his own way;

• freedom from want;

• freedom from fear.

Fifty years ago, these words resonated. Today they are just as important.

But let's add a Fifth Freedom to FDR's list–Freedom of Financial Security.

With such security, you can contribute to the financial security of your country, community, and family.

Before the Japanese economy crashed and burned in the nineties, one of the benchmarks of its prosperity was its incredible–as compared to the United States–savings rate.

We are a country of financial-planning illiterates. The concept of looking beyond today, making some adjustments so tomorrow is taken care of, often does not show up on our cultural radar screen.

Let's do something about that. Let's institute compulsory courses in financial planning, starting in high school. Teach kids early how to handle money properly. Give them more courses in college. It is sheer idiocy that we train young people to be doctors, lawyers, and Indian chiefs, but we don't bother to teach them how to take care of their finances.

They leave these institutions of higher education with a fancy diploma, but they're naked in such an utmost-important area of knowledge,

knowledge of money matters. If you don't have a clue about finances, you'll be lost for the rest of your life.

The state of Pennsylvania has been "encouraging" high school kids to take an interest in finance by sponsoring the Stock Market Game. Give the kids $100,000 of imaginary money, and let them invest in the market for twelve weeks. Whoever ends up with the most money is the winner.

So what does one senior at a tony prep school do? He takes the whole wad, drops it in one stock, and voilà, at the end of the three months he has "earned" $349,260, placing him first out of 626 participants.

And what did the young lad learn here? That the best place for long-term financial planning is in Las Vegas?

No, the best place to start is with your first paycheck or your next one. People are always saying, "When I make more money, then I'll save. I don't have enough right now."

Wrong, whatever you make is enough. Figure on putting aside from 3 to 10 percent of your total income. Take the 3 percent if you earn less than $600 a week. Increase the percentage as your salary goes up. If you make $600, what are we talking? Eighteen dollars a week. Pack and take lunch to the office. Skip some trips to the vending machine. Put off the trip to the multiplex.

If your company has a 401k plan, sign up now. It's automatic savings, with the percentage you indicate being taken out of your paycheck. Then if you're lucky, your employer contributes to it as well.

Defer the short-term pleasures for the long-term results. I coined a word many years back–squandermania. That's when you spend everything you have on things you don't need.

But wait, don't you deserve the 57-inch, wide-screen, high-definition TV? So what if it costs $2,500? Pull out the plastic. And to heck with a $10,000 Hyundai when you can have a 745i BMW sedan with a V-8 engine for $70,000. It does have front-seat knee protection, after all.

What about the protection of your present and future? If you're young with a family, don't squander money on luxuries you can't afford. Buy a life-term insurance policy to shelter your loved ones if something untoward happens to you. Ensure your future by investing wisely. Put a good portion of your investment funds in solid, principal-guaranteed instruments. You can't rely on Social Security to provide true security. Take control of your destiny to ensure dignified, comfortable, and deserved years after your prime wage-earning life ends.

Yes, thank you FDR for Social Security, but we must consider it just a floor for future well-being. We must build that well-insulated house on top of it for total financial independence.

* * *

And, very importantly, put away those credit cards.

Back in the early 1950s when a fellow named Frank X. MacNamara had the notion of a credit card, it wasn't such a bad idea. That's because charging would be for a limited use. Say you took a potential client to lunch and said client ordered the most expensive items on the menu, not to mention the three martinis.

The bill comes, and oops, you don't have enough cash. Back then, it was harder to come up with cash than it is today in the age of Automatic Teller Machines. MacNamara created the Diners Club card, where you could charge at member restaurants and get a bill at the end of the month.

Then American Express entered the field, mailing out eight million solicitations for members. From then on, there was no looking back. At the end of the sixties, BankAmericard came on the scene with a new concept. Can't pay off at the end of the month, no problem. The balance would be carried over–with interest due, of course.

Wright Patman, chairman of the House Banking Committee, in surveying the credit-card scene in 1970, after solicitations for credit cards had saturated the American market–it did not matter if you were a dachshund named Alice Griffin or you were dead, you were eligible for a card–said, "I think that the banks, ever since the moneychangers were driven out of the temple of God, have been trying to perfect some plan whereby they can collect from both sides. Credit cards have finally made that possible."

According to figures quoted by the office of the treasurer of the state of

Minnesota, "Americans carried an average credit card balance of $8,488 per household at midyear 2001, reports CardWeb.Com, a payment card information network. Considering that 85 percent of this amount accrues interest at an average rate of 15 percent, the average U.S. family is spending more than $1,000 per year in interest and fees."

How obscene is this? Credit card debt only adds to financial woes. And financial woes lead to destroyed marriages. By some estimates, fighting over money is the number one cause of divorce. And often squandermania is the underlying disease. It may be the husband, it may be the wife, but someone is out there spending too much.

I recalled a tragic case in *Milton on America*.

"There was a chap who worked two jobs to, but still was unable to come near paying off the bills his wife ran up so blithely. When he had exhausted every other loan possibility, he asked his employer to lend him money to pay off the debts. The boss, who knew the wife, said, 'What's the use? I bail you out, and she'll just do it again and again.'

"The upshot was that one day, the chap borrowed a pistol and blew his brains out. That's an extreme case, but excessive debt incurred by squandermania or for any other reason ruins millions of marriages and blights the lives of both parents and children."

Divorce is now the fourth-leading cause of bankruptcy in the U.S.

Think about it. Money problems lead to divorce, divorce to bankruptcy. A sad commentary that doesn't have to be.

*   *   *

Now you've built up a nest egg, you're not quite sure how to invest it. Friends have raved about their financial planner. My goodness, what he has done with their portfolio. Of course, even a moron does well in a bull market. Then the market tanks, and your holdings are nothing to brag about.

Keep in mind when you turn your future to these so-called planners, they may be planning their financial gain and not yours. It is an under-regulated industry. Caveat emptor. And you are the buyer.

And that is what the bottom line is. You must control your own destiny. You are the one who charges that $400 sweater you "just had to have." You are the one who makes speculative investments. You are the one who doesn't appreciate the long-term advantage of compound interest—you know, interest that is calculated not only on the initial principal, but also the accumulated interest of prior periods. It adds up. It is good.

Compound interest may not be as sexy as high-flying stocks. Solid bonds, the United States Treasury kind or the tax-free municipals where even your principal can be insured, may not earn you great cocktail-party bragging rights. But in the long run, you will be the winner with a happy and secure future.

That's what the Fifth Freedom is all about. Without it, without financial freedom, you will not be able to live a worry-free life.

Epilogue

We are in a time of great strife, of great turmoil, of great unrest.

The United States, because of the luxury of geography, has been immunized against the plagues that ravaged the world in the past. But now technology and advancements have brought the peoples of the world closer together, and we are more vulnerable.

In these perilous times of conflict, all our citizens should persevere in their efforts as a person, as a family member, and as a member of their community. In these times, we need all the energies of all our people working toward common good and civility.

We issued our Declaration of Independence in 1776. Let us issue another today. We will fight to be independent and free of those who wish us harm, who try to sabotage and obliterate the very foundation of our country. They will not succeed, no matter how heinously they try, for the foundation of the United States as so masterfully laid by our Founding Fathers will withstand all such assaults. That is as long as we, the people, remember who we are and what we stand for.

In these times, we can't risk appeasement and conciliation. If the Saddam Husseins of the world want to challenge us, let them suffer the consequences. If the Osama bin Ladens think they can distort their religious teachings into justification for attacking us, let them feel the force of our moral outrage.

And when the dust settles, we should be prepared to offer aid and direction toward establishing peace and justice. What better example of postwar success can there be than the Marshall Plan? Rather than grind the conquered into the ground, as was tried after World War I, we helped Germany and Japan rebuild and prosper and become the allies they are today.

Besides being the most powerful military force on earth, we must remember we have the most powerful ideology, as well. Let's not be afraid to spread the gospel of our Constitution, our Bill of Rights, and the American dream.

Only then can peace be with us. I trust that this book will be an inspiration for all of us for many, many years to come.

Arthur Milton
March, 2003

Index

Medicaid, 113
medical errors, 106-107
Medicare, 113
Milken, Michael, 96
Milton on America, 121, 136
Montesquieu, baron de
    (Charles Louis de Secondat), 15-16
"Mr. Rodger's Neighborhood", 70
My American Journey, 71
National Academy of Sciences, 113
National Alliance of Youth Sports,125-126
National Broadcasting Company, 68
National Highway Traffic Safety
    Administration, National Highway
    Transportation Safety Board, 96
National Institutes of Health, 69
national sales tax, 79-80
New York Infirmary for
    Women and Children, 64
New York magazine, 107
New York Times, 68
NHTSA. *See* National Highway Traffic
    Safety Administration.
NHTSA. *See* National Highway
    Transportation Safety Board.
Nixon, Richard, 106
No Child Left Behind Act, 85
Novello, Antonia Coello, 68-70
O'Connor, Sandra Day, 120
OECD. *See* Organization for Economic
    Cooperation and Development.
Operation Desert Storm, 42.
    See also Persian Gulf War.
Organization for Economic
    Cooperation and Development, 84
Paige, Rod, 84
Paine, Thomas, 8-9
Partnership for Learning, 126
Pataki, George, 70
Paterson, Shirley, 77
Patman, Wright, 135
Pearl Harbor, 37, 50

pellagra, 65-66
Penn, William, 5
Pershing, General John, 36
Persian Gulf War, 172
Piedmont Hospital, Atlanta, 109
Pilgrims, 4-5, 57
Plato, 82
Powell, Colin, 71-72
Powell, Luther, 71
Powell, Maud, 72
prescriptions, electronic, 110-111
Puerto Rico Herald, 69
Puritans, 4-5
Radiola, 68
Raleigh, Walter, 3
Raum, Arnold, 81
RCA, 68
Reagan, Ronald, 38, 78, 82
religious persecution, 4-5
Revolution of 1848, Germany, 59
Riis, Jacob, 60
road rage, 126-129
Robinson, Allen, 128
Rogers, Will, 79, 100, 115
Rolfe, John, 4
Roosevelt, Franklin Delano, 37, 61-62, 133
Roosevelt, Theodore, 35
Rosenberg, Charles E., 104
Roto Zip Tool Corporation, 98
Rowan, Carl, 71
Sara Lee Corporation, 97-98
Sarnoff, Abraham, 67
Sarnoff, David, 67-68
Savard System, 111
Savard, Marie, 111
Schoenbaum, Stephen C., 107
Schottenstein stores, 98
Schurz, Carl, 59
Serapis, H.M.S., 63
"Sesame Street", 70
Simon, William E., 81

Documents that forged a nation

Speeches for the ages

The year 1932 was a pivotal one for Arthur Milton. The country was celebrating the two-hundreth anniversary of George Washington's birth. The young Arthur took to the stage as the father of our country in a city-wide production staged by Yorkville Junior High School.

Seventy-one years later, Arthur Milton will tell you that this event instilled in him a patriotism for his country that he nourishes daily.

The author of numerous books, Mr. Milton's views on consumer-protection legislation have been published in the Congressional Record. He believes that "In this era of consumer awareness, it should be a constant teaching process so that all Americans can live wisely within their income, save and invest intelligently, and strive for dignity in their twilight years."

A former broadcaster for Armed Forces Radio, he has appeared on radio and TV and is a frequent lecturer and public speaker. For five years, Mr. Milton was a feature writer for *Financial World*. He lives in New York City with his wife, Phyllis.